DEPLORABLE

DEPLORABLE

"WE THE PEOPLE"

R.M. HARGOLD

DEPLORABLE
"WE THE PEOPLE"

iUniverse books may be ordered through booksellers or by contacting:

iUniverse
1663 Liberty Drive
Bloomington, IN 47403
www.iuniverse.com
1-800-Authors (1-800-288-4677)

Because of the dynamic nature of the Internet, any web addresses or links contained in this book may have changed since publication and may no longer be valid. The views expressed in this work are solely those of the author and do not necessarily reflect the views of the publisher, and the publisher hereby disclaims any responsibility for them.

Any people depicted in stock imagery provided by Getty Images are models, and such images are being used for illustrative purposes only. Certain stock imagery © Getty Images.

ISBN: 978-1-5320-9178-0 (sc)
ISBN: 978-1-5320-9179-7 (e)

Print information available on the last page.

iUniverse rev. date: 12/26/2019

INTRODUCTION

I couldn't help stopping for a moment, looking around at all taken for granted by all of us every moment of our daily existence. Most likely, this realization factor comes with age as I do remember my grandmother's having the same commented look back recollections of times gone past. My hometown has changed dramatically; some would call it advancement others a decline. Raised in the small city of Norwich, Connecticut, I now see a rundown town that is quite different from what I remember. A town favorite was always Vocatura's Bakery, where you can still get that dry tuna grinder on their own freshly baked bread. A quaint place that brings back the memories of my memere when we used to stop there on our way to the beach. Just up the street, the Hess gas station was still there, now gone. The same place that I remember getting the annual, limited edition Hess Truck for Christmas, sitting at the gas pump watching the windows washed, and the oil checked by the attendant. It is rare to find an attendant at a gas station nowadays who will pump your gas and wash your windows, let alone pull the dipstick or add engine oil. Dairy Queen is still in operation up in the Taftville section of town, but to say the least many others have closed, moved, or occupied by another business. So many houses have been partitioned and turned into apartments, many buildings run down. Where corn and hay fields once dominated are now condos or apartment complexes to accommodate the workers and population growth enhanced by the casinos built close to a once quiet area. Surly as I finish this book, one or more of my memories will fade and be replaced by another business or close, lying vacant like the others before them.

   With the many changes and current happenings across the nation, I can't help but empathize with those who are in the same quandary as I, asking themselves, "How did we get here"? We, as busy individuals, have been unconsciously thrust into a very volatile time in our country, propagated with so much division and hate. Each day that passes, each tweet, blog, post, interview, biased comment, our society appears to be drawing closer to the critical boiling point heated by the two polarized sides. We have liberals, conservatives, progressives, left and right to name a few of the titles placed upon those with societal or political opposing views. Many have found a division within their family units, with neighbors, friends, and casual acquaintances all seemingly in a different light or are more distant due to this last presidential election.

At no time in memory do I recollect such a political divide. We grew up with Democrats and Republicans in the family and friends of the family. There was never such a significant separation in viewpoints, especially those that are so dramatic and outwardly violent. In recollection, Democrats were for the working man or the Unions; many were from what I recall predominantly Catholic, as was my memere. Republicans favored the working folks as well; however, more so the farmers, field workers, or non-union workers, and many were from the more Evangelical Christian religions like my grandmothers, Lutheran, Episcopalian, or Baptist. A commonality to politics or the political scene was everyone had their opinions; there wasn't a far left or far right, steadfast liberal or conservative platform. Most of all, no one threatened bodily harm, damage to your property, or committed violent acts because you were of an opposing thought pattern. Those of whom I encountered were predominantly first-generation immigrants or naturalized citizens of the United States, all of whom stood by their civic duty to vote in "all" elections. Some even feared if they didn't vote, it was illegal, and they would face some form of prosecution.

Not only by personal experiences and observations, the interactions with passing strangers, offered insightful opinion and political views highlighting what has become a divided nation in need of dramatic unification through a reminder of simpler times past. Questioning of the mainstream media reporting, social media posts, and rebuttals played a significant role in the divided opinions, all needing critique and caution to the immediate belief of fact. I cannot nor expect what is within the text of this book to be in complete agreement with all who choose to read.

All I ask is to become or keep attentive to the dramatic changes around us, which require all of us to take a step back and look at our country today from outside the window glass looking in. Your open mind with eyes wide open is needed now more than any as we as a nation are at a crucial point whether we move forward from these divisive times in our soon to be history with each passing moment.

Taking you through events and personal experiences surrounding the 2016 election forward, it will become apparent how media bias has hypocritically propagated a social divide, which has caused such unrest in our nation. This exhaustive and, at times, headache driven look into what our society has become should prove alarming and prompt an overview or push for a change in the direction of the tracks as our country is on a path for a massive train wreck ahead.

The pages of history written long ago, those that should be the stories told once again, of division unified into one nation of free people. These narratives of battles won and lost must be read for a reason for their fight and the lives lost. The destruction of memorials, censorship of writings, suppression of speech, propaganda by political talking heads, and biased media, we as a nation are under attack with an agenda unknown to any of us. A plan we must be sure to reign in, as its existence has blatantly become apparent, not a positive nor benefit to us all as a sovereign nation of free people.

DEDICATION

This book has been fashionably titled and dedicated to all those forgotten, ignored, no longer heard, wonderful Americans newly named, deplorable, who still stand with courage and resilience. This book would not be possible without those millions of people who are an inspiration standing proud, like "Deplorable Deb reporting from her basket," Diamond and Silk, and those everyday Americans with strong convictions with never wavering patriotism.

Sincere thanks to Donald J Trump, his family, those in his cabinet, his stern, steadfast supporters for putting aside your everyday lives to stand up for our country and protect it from a socialist implosion.

Lastly, but most importantly, mom, my son Nicholas, husband Gary, and close friends, for your daily encouragement and nagging to get it done.

I love you all, may God bless the United States of America and watch over every one of us.

TIME FOR A NEW PRESIDENT

 ——◆——

As constitutionally written every four years, we as a nation embark on another journey to choose a leader of our country. A new sounding board or scapegoat to take the heat and blame for our, "kick the can" politicians who drag their feet from president-elect to president-elect. These procrastinating politicians are winning election after election, further becoming embedded within the roots of our government known as the "deep state." It is viewed almost not probable they could be replaced by an opponent, unless by a more aggressive agenda based control group. What our founding fathers failed to foresee was term limits needed for senators and representatives, many of whom now have been in office 40 to 50 plus years. These very politicians for life will become the divisive body that our forefathers did not intend.

I find it amazing how we have acquaintances that are average and seen as typical staunch Democrat union workers. These individuals are under no circumstances saw the problematic issues surrounding Hillary Clinton and the damage the Obama administration had done to so many people around them. Some of the old school Democrats or Union workers would never stray from the "vote Democrat" rule. It used to be taboo to drive a foreign car to the job site, buy American only mentality even though there are few if any vehicles manufactured entirely with the USA only components. Although the lifelong Democrats generally stood steadfast with their voting habits, many I spoke with did stray away, in the 2016 election voting independently and dare I mention for Trump.

Not all societal issues can be blamed solely upon the Obama administration nor Hillary Clinton. During the eight years under Obama, not only did we see a predominant dividing force, but a reinforcement or enhancement of the educational changes that shaped a new generation influenced with some highly unethical, backward, and hypocritical views. This alleged modern society with thwarted or opposing ideologies has become an imminent concern for the generations of the past now experiencing a violent, out of control hypocrisy that has become a danger for the very society we all now live. So many feared that without change the culture, America, as a unit would implode within itself and fail to exist with the common core values our founding fathers fought, died, and lobbied for under what has come under fire, our most sacred, the Constitution of the United States.

Throughout the very active presidential election year of 2016, the spectrum of views from what was now considered the left and the right were so far apart that the extremes prevailed without a central point for logical rebuttal or collective resolve. Once the candidates were chosen, and the battle began, it was no longer typical, wait and see what happens. In many views, the lesser of two evils equated to the survival or destruction of the country. I had never heard such extreme viewpoints as notable during this unprecedented election cycle in 2016. Granted, with the knowledge of the Clintons, I had no intention of voting for Hillary Clinton, even if she was a woman. Just because a woman is running for president, for the first time in history, does not mean she is qualified to do so. Is it time for a woman president? Absolutely, and many would agree, but not a woman named Hillary Rodham Clinton. What I did find astounding was the blinded following that Hillary had during this crucial moment in our country's history. My amazement continued as few could see Bernie Sanders' body language of discontent, defeat, hands together fingers extended, up toward his face, with an unmistakable look of disgust while all others around him stood cheering for the chosen Democrat nominee. This disgust in a fixed evidentiary system that put the "breaker of the glass ceiling or the true chosen one" before the desires of the people, this I found most baffling. In my mind, and the thoughts of millions, this was not a fair chosen nomination. The tides were forcefully changed in the direction that the Democrats felt the country wanted, or what was intended by agenda. How surprised all would be when their choices proved otherwise as the DNC and Hillary Clinton underestimated the real grass root voters in the country.

My husband and I were amazed that Bernie Sanders did not win the Democrat nomination, but then again, when the only two standing were Sanders and Clinton, no surprise that she was inevitably placed at the head of the table instead. Bernie preached to the hearts and minds of the millennials, who were saddled with college tuition or the lack of ability to obtain the funds necessary to attend with his "free college for all" narrative, never mentioning who ultimately was going to pay the bill. Although Bernie touched on some of the concerns of the average everyday American, he never really connected with the core concerns. The Bernie Sanders effect would be felt later in the midterm elections when his powerful platform would resonate with a new generation of incoming candidates who also preached and ultimately won on the "free for all" platform. This "free for all" platform of promises, including free education, spoke loudly to those saddled with student loan debt but went a step further, adding in "Medicare for all," another unknown, how to fund, pie in the sky campaign promise.

Hillary Clinton would consistently claim that she had a message, she would direct you to read it on her website, or we all should know what it is. The truth of the matter was, Hillary's message was no real change other than a woman would be in the top position of power in the White House, and a vote for her is only for her. The "I'm With Her" advertising promotion began with a thought, comment then a logo of a capital "H" with a side to side arrow. This initial advertisement would be the first of many seen on bumper stickers, t-shirts, email headers, and candidate promotional propaganda. What Hillary didn't seem to realize her past actions, deeds, previous and current comments, narcissism, and condescension for millions of voters would haunt and control the outcome of her candidacy. Hillary would be one of the most disconnected candidates observed by a vast majority of the legal voting public. Hillary failed to connect with the American voter on the concerns over illegal alien immigration, welfare reform, vetting of refugees, job growth, manufacturing, healthcare issues, veteran's affairs, high taxation, and enormous debt. The average American could barely afford their mortgages, had to make choices between a mortgage payment on their home, or pay their healthcare premiums that skyrocketed under the unaffordable affordable healthcare act (ACA) or Obamacare. The candidate, Hillary Clinton, made a poor choice in words and went as far as to tell hundreds of already hurting miners in West Virginia that they would be out of their current jobs due to clean energy advancements. Without offering other financial stability options other than government-subsidized funding, regretfully, she had to walk back her comments. What Hillary neglected to understand workers want to be workers, they want to pay for and provide for their families themselves, not be indebted to the government. Most Americans are too proud to take a handout and were raised that welfare was unacceptable and an absolute last resort, not a way of life.

I am marginally biased to Hillary Clinton. However, I still wished to afford her the benefit of the doubt. Perhaps, she may have a possible solution to the multitude of issues our country faces and has been in office or around the areas that can institute change; she may have some valid ideas. Not the case. Hillary didn't have a message of positive change for the American people, only a strong desire to be in control and maintain the status quo in governmental ineptitude. The fact was Hillary Clinton was a career politician, and career politicians were one of the very problematic issues in this country that need attention. Hillary was good at appeasing and appealing to her base followers by targeting the heartstrings of being a mother and grandmother. When offended would attempt to divert attention from her personal and political issues, she would play with "woman card" and accuse those who disagreed as being misogynistic. During the 2016 election, the DNC sent mass emails to all presumed to be in support affording one the ability to sign up for a "woman card" with a donation, of course. Really?

When Hillary was due to speak in Connecticut as a presidential candidate, I did sign up for tickets to hear her speak. Since then, I have been inundated with propaganda from the DNC and Democrats, further keeping me in the loop of what they are telling their voting base and what direction they wish the country to head. As I listened to Hillary's publicized speeches, comments, accusations, and ultimate condescending criticisms of the American people she claimed to represent, she never realized that she was alienating herself further away from millions of those still on the fence, independent of party loyalty. One of her greatest moments and best criticisms of the everyday average American voter was the day she was video captured calling so many that were not her supporters those that belonged in a basket, or the "Basket of Deplorables." Millions of voters, newly segregated by Hillary Clinton, began wearing the insult as a badge of honor. The same aware voters were vowing they would not allow an insulting, condescending, narcissistic woman who felt entitled to the presidency, enter the office. It would be a vote for Trump or no one.

All political candidates must be able to sell themselves, enticing voters including; Democrat, Republican, Independent, veterans, impoverished, elite, rich and poor, to vote for them. The presumption of the outcome will surprise you, and entitlement is never guaranteed. Although a popularity contest, even the most popular, is not the most liked. Her failure to connect with those who had valid concerns about their safety and future, further alienating them by insult would prove to be her demise and thus prevent her from ever entering the White House and be seated as "madam president." Hillary should have listened to Bill Clinton; she claimed her political advisor, who was a former president, the first Democrat elected to two consecutive terms, and a was likable even with his shortcomings. Bill Clinton knew how to connect with the American people, was known for many positive changes during his presidency. Although he was remembered by many for his negatives, those negatives were minimal to his successes as a leader of the country. Bill did advise Hillary where to campaign, and to her ultimate demise, she ignored his advice, going off on her own, which led to failure.

Hillary's failures stemmed decades; however, only those in recent tabloids, media segments, and memories of the American people played a large roll in her loss of the electorate. Hillary Clintons' work record as Secretary of State regarding Benghazi, Libya, Uranium One, her callousness with email security resounded with millions. Another Clinton scandal added to the list of questionable dealings from the misappropriated funding to Haiti, which were nothing in comparison to the influx of millions of dollars to the Clinton Foundation during her tenure in office and candidacy by foreign governments. The same foreign governments which donated were those that suppressed the rights of women of whom she fervently claimed to lobby for standing up as an advocate for women's rights. The clincher would be her general condescending nature to others. It would be her downfall against the most imperfect of men who had a message and connection to the people, her Republican opponent, Donald J Trump.

The look back upon the eight years of the Obama administration had been quite a section in history, one of which so many will see very differently from each other. Some will look at it as a milestone, one which elected the first black or politically correct African American to the White House for two terms in office. I did vote for Obama in his first term. I did not vote for him in the second although, I was still curious to see what direction he would continue to lead the country in and what changes may be as his first term was a bit lackluster. Speaking to many, some had thought that he would bring a considerable shift in the suppressed, mostly black communities, ending poverty and affording more opportunities for advancement. The candidate elected President Obama stood on the platform of immigration reform, border security, equality, fair trade, and choice. Obama, unlike Clinton, campaigned on the desires of the American people, heard the needs cried out. Sound familiar? If you go back into the archives, the promises, although not kept, made by Obama were much like those of Trump. To date, President Trump has kept more campaign promises than any other elected official, even with the #resistance, obstructionist movement. Some felt that Obama would be the change agent; others like myself would take a wait and see approach. Much to the disappointment of many this change agent although, quite astute and well versed, proved to be a terrific speaker while lacking in strength to be a leader of what the strongest nation on earth. Many and Obama himself would disagree with my statement; the opposite holds to belief as well.

With failed international policies and loophole-filled national safety operations, many of my fellow Americans, and I began to feel that we were becoming a weak nation with less security and safety. Our country was now receiving an overwhelming influx of refugees of whom did not opt willingly to come to our country, were poorly vetted with some not at all. Post 9/11, there was already a stereotypical attitude toward those from predominantly Muslim countries, a fear of their ideologies and beliefs that caused concern amongst many. In 2011 a slowing or easing of visas issued to Iraqi refugees was instituted by the Obama administration post radicalization found regarding two individuals in Kentucky. Even with concerns, the vetting procedures didn't change much, and we began to encounter more instances regarding individuals carrying out attacks on American citizens by those radicalized or taught to hate, in the name of Allah. Two tragedies that validated the terrorist concerns of the American people, December 2, 2015, in San Bernardino, California 14 people, were intentionally shot, killed, while 22 others injured. With another tragic event on June 12, 2016, when 50 people died, including the shooter and 53 wounded at the Pulse Nightclub shooting in Orlando, Florida, which was a predominantly gay nightclub and considered an atrocity by this radicalized individual in the name of Allah. We as Americans came to know how much radical groups hated the beliefs and values of America, especially on 9/11, which was one of our most tragic events in history, where radicalization of a group of individuals took the lives of; 2,996 including the 19 terrorists. These attacks implanted a validated fear into the minds of all Americans, and they looked to their government leaders to protect them from further atrocities, which became a blinding reality not to come to fruition. Millions of Americans began to feel less safe as time moved on. This very paragraph outlines yet another reason why so many stayed away from Hillary Clinton and favored Donald J Trump as the preferred next president.

On September 20th, 2015, John Dickerson interviewed then-candidate Hillary Clinton on Face the Nation, where she proclaimed her favor for the United States to increase the number of refugees from Syria taking the total from 10,000 to 65,000 or more immediately due to the current humanitarian crisis. This powerful statement from her alarmed millions as our vetting process was already proven flawed. On the other side of the spectrum, then-candidate Donald J Trump in his campaign rally talking points vowed to uphold the travel ban implemented by Obama, until an extreme vetting process was created, with more protections against those questionable or unable to be vetted, trying to enter the United States with an alleged intent to harm.

One must sit back and think why the U.S. is, being targeted by radicalized groups when all that has been done or given by way of a perceived helping hand? We could contemplate if the targets on our country are due to our constant intervention and forced freedom-based ideologies that were the opposite of theirs for centuries, the countries' old beliefs, whether societal or religious based. Many radicals would rather destroy their opponent than comply with the unwelcomed changes they promote. Did we, in all actuality, bring these radical terrorist actions upon ourselves with our democratic ways? What makes us more to the right than others? We should ask ourselves, are we saving the world, or are we propagating violence? I look around at my immediate peaceful surroundings and then view the protests around our nation and find it hard to believe that we are the example of freedom to be the most excellent example for all others around the globe. We advocate for rights, and those given rights use them to promote violence and unrest. We have women advocating for freedoms and choices by walking around in crowds dressed as vaginas or with pussy hats upon their heads. What is the point of this fashion fad? How can you be seriously taken as admirable when you dress up like idiots not only embarrassing yourselves, but the country further showing we need to address civility on our stage of protest in a different manner to reach a level of validity.

During Bill Clinton's presidency, the Iranian government was in the process of nuclear advancements. Then-president Clinton and the general public knew that they would not cease even with the current sanctions and frozen assets. The transpiring of Iranian failures to comply should not have come as any surprise that when then-President Barack Obama opted to allow financial access to the Iranians, releasing the decades-old frozen assets, and enter into a questionable agreement the public would not approve. Many on social media would comment that the funds released were assets of the Iranians, and it was not an issue. However, the alleged accrued interest paid was, as it was by way of taxpayer dollars. Many did not believe in the reasoning behind why the Barack Obama administration did what it did, it was looked at as a payoff for the release of hostages, although denied by the administration, and a slippery slope allowing the Iranian government the funds to continue their nuclear advancements in the region which inevitable has come to fruition.

Much like the Bill Clinton administration policies, the Barack Obama administration was also interested in decreasing our military through funding, depletion of assets, and what was termed by Barack Obama as a "leaning." Most Americans believe you achieve peace through strength and not weakness, much like the views back during the mid-1990s when Bill Clinton and Congress began to cut military funding and to propose the closures of military bases. These actions of the time were viewed negatively and perceived as making America vulnerable to its adversaries. As a college student in Virginia during this time, I can speak first-hand of the effects the Clinton administrations' cuts were having on the Newport News area military members and families along with the surrounding regions negatively both economically and psychologically.

Where Hillary Clinton failed to see the concerns of many Americans, her opponent Donald J Trump saw and heard the pleas. Where Barack Obama vowed a leaning of military strength and Hillary Clinton showed little opposition to do the same, Donald J Trump vowed rebuilding technology and increasing military power. Where Barack Obama and Hillary both failed the American people on immigration reform, Donald J Trump promised to push for a wall on the southern border, extreme vetting bans from predominantly Muslim countries with known terrorist cells, all talking points which resonated with millions. For these contrasting views, candidate Trump, elected President Trump, and his supporters or anyone who praised these thoughts, opinions, or concerns would become the newly labeled racists, bigots, and scum of society. Somewhat hypocritical as almost all politicians and even Hillary Clinton herself can be notable throughout their political history as claiming the same concerns with vows to change, of course, during an election cycle.

Many elected politicians in the Democrat party began to preach on a "we are the world" philosophy, many of whom became more globalist than being concerned with the concerns of the American public at home. Barack Obama also became more of an advocate of helping the world before the concentration of those at home, along with his believed to be or intended successor Hillary Clinton. To the contrary of all, Donald J. Trump, commanded his audience every time with the total opposite, taking an "America First" agenda and platform for secure borders, extreme vetting, and mass deportation of illegal aliens in our country.

When it came to the Affordable Healthcare Act (ACA) or more commonly termed, Obamacare, this single-payer healthcare system, some were happy with, others appalled, candidate Trump preached changes, choices, repeal and replace. My family was one included with those millions disgruntled by what then-President Barack Obama spoke fervently with the definite selling point for this medical insurance program stating, "you can keep your plan, you can keep your doctor," both positions that became non-existent to millions. Blindly our elected Democrat politicians voted for this insurance program on the trust platform and direction of the speaker, Nancy Pelosi, who was seen and heard stating, "you have to vote on it, to see what is in it." Hindsight those politicians who were elected to serve all Americans should be apologetic to the millions burdened by the high costs incurred, however instead, the Democrat Party would preach at their podiums that 23 million people had affordable healthcare. Lacking in the political rhetoric was the acknowledgment of the balance of the general populous or an estimated 300 plus million people. Many hardworking Americans either lost care or no longer could afford their new insurance premiums and out-of-pocket deductibles. Many didn't realize, only to find out later that by accepting the expanded Medicaid, which is a government-funded or state reimbursed program, you placed your home, assets, possible inheritance, or litigation windfall on the line for future seizure by the State or Government. This probable lien on your estate was in the fine print that many political sales agents and lobbyists for this program failed to inform the purchasers. With such a debilitated country, many without jobs, struggling to make ends meet, this alleged affordable option seemed like a godsend to many only to be a trojan horse filled with problems. The ACA came with an individual mandate which forced you to either sign up and pay up or face a fine. Many reluctantly were required to pay up only to find themselves in a position where they couldn't maintain their daily necessities in addition to the high-cost insurance premiums. Some specified that they would alternate between mortgage payments and insurance premiums, others just opted out entirely. For those saddled with the new high-cost premiums coupled with a high deductible were now forced to pay more than the calculated poverty level. Now ask yourself, how does that work?

I filled out the form through our state's Access Health Program when open enrollment came around. I implemented the information for my family and me, clicked through each section, and came up with what appeared to be a reasonable quote, however, had a hefty out-of-pocket deductible. Just out of curiosity, I went back a few steps and removed the checkmark that specified, "accept subsidies," what an exciting surprise, my premium skyrocketed. Granted before Obamacare, my family paid $326.00 per month for insurance premiums with an out-of-pocket of $2500, somewhat reasonable, post-Obamacare a similar plan option with an increased out-of-pocket premium went to, $1524.00 per month and a $10,000 deductible. What many didn't realize was that by accepting the subsidies, you might get a lower rate by putting your assets at risk of future lien or seizure by the State or Federal Government. All the ACA turned out to be was a subsidy or welfare, something millions were too proud to take or didn't want. Much to my surprise, so many that I interacted with had no clear understanding of what Medicaid was or had some off the wall explanation.

A typical Democrat promise made consistently is something for less or for free, never stating what should be obvious, someone always pays. Where did anyone think the money for the subsidies would come from, we as a country are already trillions of dollars in debt? In part, those who opted not to accept the subsidies were paying a much higher premium and out-of-pocket expense. The catch to this additional premium expense was in effect its use by subsequently being afforded to other individuals with lower subsidy accepted incentives.

I ultimately refused either; I opted not to pay the high premiums and refused to pay the mandated fines, stating to those who would call to solicit program options that penalties and forced healthcare requirements were unconstitutional, and it was my right to refuse. Nothing ever came of it either way until some years later when in 2018, U.S. District Justice Reed O'Connor, in Fort Worth, Texas, ruled that the individual mandate was unconstitutional going in contradiction with Supreme Court Justice Roberts' comment that the individual mandate was a tax therefore allowed in 2012. As the individual participation mandate was met aggressively with conflicting views, it did become part of our annual federal tax filing, thus presenting as a tax upholding the opinion of Justice Roberts. This individual tax or mandate was never fully implemented as a charge or deduction from your refund when the tax filing format inevitably changed with a question and answer, yes or no, for each month you could not afford healthcare, followed by an online comment that you are not required to pay. To this day, I will still hold firm that anything pushed to the American people that cause them undue financial burden or hinders their right to a healthy life by the government and is mandated is unconstitutional. To name it a tax further pushes us backward in time to the age of the Boston Tea Party era. We as a country cannot continue down this path of increase in taxation. There is only so much that the American taxpayer can burden by the hand of inept politicians' rule before they stand up and revolt as they have in the past.

Healthcare is another place where Hillary Clinton didn't connect with millions, and Donald J Trump did. Many didn't realize that Obamacare was in concept similar to the once discarded brainchild of Hillary Clinton from back in the 1990s known as Hillarycare and turned down by then-President Bill Clinton as being ridiculous and wouldn't work. Much like the same comment he made in a speech during her 2016 presidential candidacy again stating, "it is the craziest thing he ever heard of." Another area that Donald J Trump addressed concerns from the American people, knowing that they were struggling and vowed to repeal and replace this healthcare atrocity for millions more who lost or couldn't afford care than those who obtained it.

We all know today that Obamacare has failed on its own, although the Democrat platform is Armageddon, and with the repeal of the individual mandate, we all surely are going to die, especially those with pre-existing conditions. The Democrat platform is not one of the choices, although they preach, freedom of choice, they neglect to add the stipulation by saying with governmental oversight.

Now in a country that has struggled to raise themselves from oppression, why would you want to be suppressed or controlled by a government entity ever again? The simple answer is; keep the people enabled and dependent; they will be controllable and compliant. Without saying these exact words, Hillary Clinton has always been about control, and anyone who has paid attention would have made a note of it. Donald J Trump again promoted freedom of choice and the right to choose, which is every American citizens' given right, another talking point that resonated with the voter.

The discussion of handouts, welfare, subsidies has always been a talking point for many, more so now than ever. Hardworking Americans are tired of going to work every day working hard to make ends meet, paying their bills, while their neighbor is on welfare, drives a better or newer vehicle than they do, illegal aliens or refugees receive healthcare, housing, and more benefits than the hardworking American can afford. The average American is tired of there being more takers than makers in this country. Hillary Clinton, as a candidate and a majority of those in the Democrat party of today, believes in we should "give it away," philosophy, never thinking of how much harder the average American must work to afford the higher taxation needed to provide these handouts and entitlements.

Donald J Trump, on the other hand, believes in "work for welfare." If someone is capable of working, they should, the government will still offer limited assistance but no longer allow the complete freeride — obviously, a mind-blowing concept for the opposition. Although Hillary Clinton didn't fully embrace the "Medicare for All" platform that was preached by her Democrat opponent Bernie Sanders, this platform terminology would become a wordplay for all other Democrat candidates to follow the 2016 election, now resounding loudly in the lead to the 2020 election cycle. From expanded Medicaid to Medicare for All, the concept is still the same with the inevitable outcome of being fiscally burdensome on the hardworking taxpayer.

Another extreme opposite was the controversial debate regarding Pro-Life versus Pro-Choice. Hillary Clinton has been noted to deny that a fetus is not a person with rights while in the womb and unborn. The question remains regarding her views on late-term abortions as it has changed throughout the years dependent upon the campaign talking point needed to win the vote. Although the debate always comes with heavy rebuttals from both sides and one that will not likely end soon regarding abortion. Hillary Clinton was the Pro-Choice or woman's right to choose candidate, wanting every woman to have the option to do what she so wishes with her own body, including the right to exterminate a viable fetus by way of abortion. Donald J Trump was the candidate of Pro-Life while agreeing that a woman does have the right to choose what she does with her being; it is morally unethical to take a life or abort a viable fetus.

Regardless of the beliefs or views of each candidate, they could not be more different from the other. The two presidential candidates of 2016 were as polarized as the country had become. I am one of those millions who am thankful every day that Hillary Clinton is not the current president of the United States. Although I have great empathy for our county, I am disgusted by the turmoil that it has fallen into at the wills of political propagandists with an unhealthy agenda. We are a sad example of a country to the world, contrary to what others would think or view, not because Donald J Trump became the president of the United States but, because of the forced division propagated by rhetorical political talking heads and opinion biased media play.

Regardless of political bias, the Democrat Party of today has become the staff that divides the waters in the same manner as Moses did, however, the destination of the path between is uncertain. In discussing the concerns, likes, dislikes, and hopes of many people in this country, I have found that so many feel the same or in similarity to myself. We all have seen our past float away replaced only by memories of times gone by, our rights being stripped away one by one with the perception of being flippantly ridiculed and condemned for our innate desire for the American dream or hopes for the future. We see the hard battles fought, hard work, and diligence of our founding fathers and ancestors torn away bit by bit. What was once a proud time in family history as they made the journey to the "free world" known as America, becoming financially solvent, proudly standing for the American flag and taking a vow of allegiance to their new country as naturalized citizens, now is seemingly irrelevant and no longer substantive.

The land that afforded such prospects and opportunities was becoming trivial or inconsequential. We were being forced to give up or fight for our rights, religious convictions, beliefs, and the right to openly express those beliefs. Our children were no longer learning of America, the history, the battles, strides, and progressions. The wants of one now supersede the needs or likes of many, whereas we could not even say "Merry Christmas" to one another because it would offend someone who didn't believe in it, therefore, suppressed to; "Happy Holidays." To some, the view of stating

"Happy Holidays" encompassed all the holidays during the season, others sheer laziness, some lack in Christianity, and suppression of belief. Each of us with our reasoning. Fact is, the tens of thousands to the millions across the country, many of whom attended the Trump rallies then and now, rejoice when the comment is made, "We will now say, Merry Christmas again."

Failures upon the system, and oversight of radicals, those suffering from aggressive behaviors or mental health issues, of whom commit atrocities with firearms, now threaten our rights to bear arms constitutionally. The overall significance and meaning of our very constitution were being nullified and changed before our eyes by the indoctrination of new thought and purpose. This time unlike any other time in our history was crucial; we no longer as a nation could allow the threads of our democracy to be unraveled. We needed a real change agent, one who would be substantial, stand up for us, and put America first and foremost before any other. In the 2016 election, it was the time for the pied piper, and his message resounded loud and clear. Donald J Trump, spoke to the people, like the people, and sold himself to be for the people, as it should be.

Donald J Trump was nor is a perfect man and has his faults. However, he was and is a true believer in America and what this country was presumed to become by our founders, and not only has he received blowback, his supporters have as well. I can't help but wonder the PTSD effects that may be felt by the Trump family post-presidency as they are absolutely under fire at every turn, as well as their supporters of whom speak so loudly now without suppression any longer. Most are getting accosted and feel the backlash by the opposing leftist propagandist viewpoints and actions; however, the soul of the patriot is hardcore and will awaken to defend.

RESPECT

—◄◆►—

If you look in the dictionary, the actual meaning of respect is a far cry from what has been either taught of misrepresented to many of our youth today and one primary fact which I'm sure many will agree. From the outward actions by many during protests to the media misrepresentations and comments made on-air or via social media, respect is nonexistent unless you are validating or agreeing to specified views or opinions. If you disagree, it is an infringement of their "freedom of speech" or first amendment rights. To differ now in this new era of confusion, you are disrespectful, ignorant, bias, intolerant, or psychologically imbalanced, needing to seek professional help, whether correct or not. Indoctrinated or propagated perception of a viewpoint or meaning outweighs the actuality of reality today.

Much of the new view or action of respect for oneself or another is to blame with the many changes in family life coupled with the outside of the home influences. How many remember the spankings, cat n' nine tails, the board pointer from class, the principal's office, or even an element of fear of being punished when you got home, anxious that the school may have called your parents? Generally, the offense was menial where you didn't do your homework, set off fireworks in the bathroom, talked too much in class, or better yet opted to cut class.

Most kids over the past 20 years have now been enabled or conditioned on how to rule the roost. Someone who thought they knew all regarding child-rearing, came along, got a group of individuals together and lobbied to protect the children no matter the circumstances. As if parenting or the occasionally disciplinary methods were not enough, kids were being instructed or taught in school that if your parent spanks you, threatens, or you feel threatened, you have the right to call 911 or the police and have your parent arrested. Sounds quite ludicrous, doesn't it? However, it happened and still does, making parents apprehensive or sometimes afraid to discipline their children and letting them do as they please, creating their own set of rules and values. Out the window goes respect, don't talk back to your parents, respect your elders, most importantly, actual actions and meaning of respect. I have heard the comments made by the child to their elder or adult disciplinarian that their boundaries or disciplinary actions were not showing the child respect; therefore, they, in turn, do not deserve respect. Mind-boggling, isn't it?

Another, quality teach your child the value of discipline was then put them in the corner, which was found to segregate, alienate, and cause too much emotional harm, ridicule by others, so they came up with the "love" or "hug it out" theory of positive reinforcement. How does this work? Your child acts out against discipline in an effort by the parent or adult to be taught or reiterated boundaries, and you hug it out, telling them how much you love them?

As human beings, we generally seek companionship, acceptance, and affection so what are you saying to the child is, act out of control, be mean, scream, cry, pull a temper tantrum and you will receive love and affection with a constant verbalization, "I love you." No wonder they are confused when they act out as young adults and get arrested or become repeat violent offenders because of no recourse or understanding of boundaries. Granted, understandably, some people took the heavy hand aspect of discipline quite a bit too far and some child advocacy groups needed to step in, however, when they blanketed the entire parental population with ramifications, they created what we have now is a generation of out of control, spoiled, unruly kids or young adults.

Unfortunately for most now, young adults or those still in school barely could manage without an I-Phone, ATM card (consistently funded by mom or dad), fast food restaurants, or a microwave. You can, with obvious definition, tell those who were brought up with the so titled non-compliant parents or the ever so terrible old ways versus the new generation of "I want them to have a better life than I did," ideology.

As a hypothetical experiment to validate my theory to this blatantly sad circumstance of child-rearing, you could place two sets of young adults in a wilderness setting or off the grid scenario, and the prominent survivor will be those taught by those "terrible old ways" or non-conforming parents. I pride myself as having shown my son to be able to live off the grid and by the land, as one day the lights may not turn on, or we will become a cashless society where those who rely on the credit card, debit card, and the bottomless money pit, will be at a loss, unable to function. Oh, the drama will be.

As of late with manipulation and prompting from media outlets, social media platforms, and #resist political talking heads, the sheep of this movement rise to an action in protest of what they do not know the reason. Protesters of today only know that they have been led to believe their protest crucial to the survival of humanity. When asked what most are protesting or resisting, they either offer no comment or begin shouting, chanting, aggressively to divert from the matter, therefore, affirming the belief they have no idea why. I have entertained many a debate, some stay on a consistent civil tone with valid points stated, others generally fly off the rails of reasoning. When dealing with individuals imbued with a tunneled thought pattern the interaction ultimately ends with the typical comments; "you're a bot, Russian bot, moron, stupid idiot," and much more profane comments which I'm sure anyone reading this would know precisely what feedback choices I am referring.

The level of disrespect in this country is unlike anything I have experienced in my lifetime. Those who are the ultimate abusers of "over the top" disrespect for another hide behind the belief that it is their given right under the United States Constitution, and they are displaying their right to free speech. What they don't realize is freedom of speech does have its boundaries, and it is not to cause undue harm, distress, or incite violence toward another party. Unnecessary damage and suffering can be looked at from both sides, as one who protests with slanderous comments or violent outbursts is invading the rights of the other. However, the one committing the outbreaks become instantaneously angered by their perception of those believed rights violated, when confronted with a logical debate. The vicious cycle will be a hard one to break as it has taken a generation to create. This confusion of freedoms meaning is where a politicians' rhetoric and media play come into the balance, which in this current social environment is all but civility nonexistent. We have opinion media with seemingly endless talking heads that offer their one-sided perspective on every subject matter, putting forward their best efforts of suggestive reasoning to the viewer. Dependent upon the individuals' background and understanding of a subject matter, this indicative reasoning can thwart the view of the one listening to this talking head. By observance of the insurmountable comments made by those on social media outlets, one can determine where the conflicting information originated, and many times the informational contradictions can be led to which mainstream media source. Too many times, the information has been presented unfairly, without confirmation, and tend to lack in historical fact. When you interact with these individuals and present historical data, you are shut down, called moronic, or have partaken in too much "Trump Koolaid." Sometimes the contradictions and cluelessness are concerning, where you ask yourself, what in the world have these people been taught, realizing that perhaps you and others across this country should have paid closer attention over the past couple of decades or more. Regardless of the stark facts, we are here now and must deal with what lies before us all.

We have a gentleman of whom we call, "the Democrat." He is a staunch Democrat, whose world view is predominantly based biased by what he hears via the radio, the MSNBC commentator, Rachel Maddow, enamored by him and other media heads he may listen to with predominantly left-leaning ideologies. He favors CNN and MSNBC. Although, he listens to Rush Limbaugh, and claims he does so to know how crazy the Republicans are and what they are doing or up to next.

Because my husband, my son, and I all voted for Trump in the 2016 election, we are now Republicans in his eyes, even though we are all registered independent and do vote for some Democrats in elections, dependent upon their stand on the issues within our state. The 2016 election has placed a strain on the relationship with our longtime acquaintance and his wife.

He has told us we are not worldly, uneducated, and the box we listen to is wrong, this referral to my cellphone, television, or the internet on our computers. According to our well-informed Democrat, we know nothing about the country and world, are consistently, stupidly and egregiously misled by Fox news. Every instance when the Trump administration accomplishes something, he tells us it is a lie because he knows it is so, the story told him so. Most recently, he even used the Trump Koolaid comment and specified that he thought we were smarter than we are and was disappointed in us. With respect, we generally, don't bother with rebuttal as this man is unfortunately illiterate and doesn't read nor write well, he was a product of his societal atmosphere many years ago much to his detriment today, which makes him the prime candidate for the unfair brainwashing that is being put forward to so many today. Having been dropped through the educational cracks, he was able to manage, entering the military briefly, securing a union position as a machine operator early on, then retiring when he was middle-aged. Although mechanically inclined with expertise in this field, he cannot still make choices or evaluations without some direction and unable to read or comprehend without assistance. Ironically, this same man will vote democrat, say the Democrats are running the state or country well, the Democrats do no wrong because they are for the people, he supports his democrat run state yet travels across state lines to buy gas because it is cheaper. His spouse just recently retired from a negotiating position within the union and is an avid reader, who received an honorary degree from UConn without undertaking the same effort that many of us took years to achieve and thousands of dollars in student loans to pay. As they say, opposites attract by the likenesses they have in common. Both being of retirement age, they were able to obtain positions with union shops early in their working years, affording them the retirement they have today, which could be considered their dominant likeness. Their difference is blatantly apparent by the political knowledge presented by each. He repeats the same talking points that he hears, without the fore or afterthought of fact to fiction, she has the same thought patterns of the old democrats, legal immigration, fair pay, opposed to high taxation, opposite of the new era democrats of today. Regardless, if the candidate has a "D" after it, they have the vote, good, bad, or otherwise.

Times were good back when both of our acquaintances and others knew the Democrat party indeed was a representative of the working class, and the country was moving forward, unlike to stagnant pace of the past decade or so, especially within our state of Connecticut. Although we have encountered vast differences in political opinion or thought, we still value each other as good acquaintances despite our hyper-exaggerated political differences in this era of polarization. Whether it be us with our acquaintances, family members, friends, or counterparts, we all have our strengths and weaknesses, educational backgrounds, or lack thereof. We are all still in this together, to prosper or fail, although failure is a matter of opinion.

How our interactions refer to the subject of respect is that although we disagree on our election choices, political views, outlook on our country's future, we are still respectful of our differences. We are just as stubbornly opinionated as they are being outspoken many a time, even with a strained relationship, we remain on the common ground although now seen in a different personal light.

When Sarah Huckabee Sanders was asked to leave a restaurant named the Red Hen in Lexington, Virginia, only because of her position in the White House as press secretary for the current Trump administration, an unlevel plain of respect the nation witnessed through this evident hypocrisy of actions toward another. As cited by multiple news organizations, the co-owner, Stephanie Wilkinson, was contacted at home the night that Sarah and her entourage met for dinner at this eatery by waitstaff of whom allegedly stated they were uncomfortable with serving this group. Ms. Wilkinson not being present at the time, opted to return to her restaurant, addressed, and pulled Sarah aside privately to express the displeasure of her position and those of the administration, subsequently asking all in the party to leave the establishment. One of the workers noted to have taken a pride photo posting it on social media as a win, win. This win, win short-lived when the backlash began over this unethical request. It was reported later and confirmed by former Governor Mike Huckabee that Sarah and her husband opted to go home, while the remaining guests in her party went to another eatery across the street and were subjected to a chanting crowd outside of the restaurant further disrupting their meal as well as others. A continued protest allegedly, organized by the co-owner of the Red Hen, Stephanie Wilkinson. Ironically, the Red Hen in Lexington, Virginia, has a sign posted on the exterior of their establishment that reads as such; "Love is the only force capable of transforming an enemy into a friend." Words of the great Dr. Martin Luther King, Jr. A mere contradiction and hypocrisy showed by the actions of disrespect by this shop owner and her staff.

The argument has been made by those who defend the actions of the Red Hen Restaurant, staff, and owner, was that the Trump administration placed a ban on transgender people in the military, therefore hated the LGBTQ community as a unit. Another viewed misconception propagated by politicians and the media.

The case involving Sarah Sanders and her party was unlike that of the Colorado baker refusal, whereas this was an everyday group of people getting together for dinner subsequently and critically condemned for Sarah's job choice. The Huckabee family are devout Christians with deep-rooted religious beliefs and values; they did not shun this restaurant because it had gay individuals working there; they didn't cast stones and were respectful. Some commenters on social media cited the 14th amendment and how this was the grounds for validation of these actions taken by the establishment. To the contrary, the posting of a "win, win" by the staffer, the request to leave based upon political bias, and the subsequent protest harassment across the street, falls into the blatant disrespect for another, undue harm and stress. In no way is this freedom of speech, peaceful coexistence, nor civility.

The events surrounding the Red Hen Restaurant, Sarah Sanders, the guests, staff members, and owners, were that representative of blatant overly reactive actions which could have been accepted in part if the situation of conflicting political views and were handled more diplomatically with less childish actions hiding behind the first amendment. As the party was already seated, had received their first course, the service should have continued. When the server or servers refused to do their job or were uncomfortable, then the owner should step in and take the service or have another server proceed in their place. The Red Hen staffer allowed to ridicule the event on social media, and the owner herself showed a lack of sound business judgment and social civility when she organized an additional outward action with a protest outside of a fellow restaurant with a blatant attempt to harass all inside.

The need for an element of respect for another or common ground understanding of another's religious conviction is exemplified as a separation of church and state by the Supreme Court ruling on the Colorado baker case in a 7-2 margin. Through sheer determination and fight for his rights to freedom of religion, this man just about bankrupted himself to achieve his goal and defend his rights. A devout Christian having raised in a very religious setting, marriage has always been between a man and a woman, has been for centuries, and so it is written in the oldest history book known to man, the Bible. Being a pastry chef myself, I, too, have been faced with questionable or controversial circumstances or requests. However, each application is never the same and needs to be deemed appropriate at the time. In the case of Jack Phillips, he is a creative cake designer, and when your product is exceptional, you tend to be in demand. Although he had supplied innovative designs for a gay couple on more than one occasion, he felt the need to decline when asked to create a wedding cake for a union between gay partners. As his firm Christian belief was that this was an institution between a man and woman, one of which he held deep and true within his Christian values he respectfully declined and was met with what would turn out to be a nightmare of criticism, slander, disrespect, and condemnation by public opinion. The gay couple opted to push the narrative that they were being discriminated against and sued Phillips, which in turn ultimately led to the Supreme Court and a legal ruling in favor of Phillips based upon religious freedoms granted under the U.S. Constitution.

Although understandable, the gay couple would desire a fabulous creation for their union. However, they also should have respected the religious convictions of the baker when he refused on this one event, although another bakery may have been willing to provide services for the event without concern nor compromise to their core values and religious beliefs, the couple insisted on compliance from one locale. Respect happens both ways, so does compromise. An unfortunate division that has come about with many who feel they should be accepted and acknowledged at all costs, without consideration for those who are not willing to or their convictions tell them otherwise. We could look at all circumstances, evaluate both examples, and attempt to find common ground. However, those in opposition or what is now termed the liberal left will have no part of any compromise.

In the circumstances of the baker, he was open about his religious convictions, and this should have warranted respect and appreciated by the couple with an understanding. He had provided cakes for other events which were of no issue for him and did not offer any conviction to his beliefs. Therefore, he was not discriminatory. When presented with confliction and his firm Christian values were in play, he had every right to refuse and ask them to go elsewhere. The couple should have respected his religious beliefs and taken the high road, with common ground understanding and appreciation.

Many Americans are tired of being forced to believe or accept much of what is unacceptable to them or in violation of their religious beliefs or values. Granted, throughout history, we have developed and worked past many segregations, racial, or personal sexual-oriented issues. Those who ride with "coexist" bumper stickers should understand what it specifies. We all can exist together, but only through respect for one another. Too many groups play the race or discrimination card attempting to beat down or force their values or existence upon another. It should be acceptable to "agree to disagree," then move on, hence, coexistence.

Most do not care who you sleep with, what color your hair is, if today you are a man, tomorrow you are a woman, or perhaps you are unsure and can't make up your mind, therefore non-binary. Most care little of other individuals' personal choices, provided they are not forced to believe or accept what they find offensive, against their core values, or religious convictions. People should take pride in themselves without making a spectacle while doing it, and if a display is what you seek for validation, it is not for everyone to applaud if not entertained nor interested.

Recently, political talking heads, namely, Maxine Waters of California, decided to go on another tirade, calling for push back to those who work for the Trump administration or are in the cabinet, no matter where they are, making sure they know they are not welcome. Any logically minded individual would look at this as inciting violence, divisive, and highly unethical for a public official. As the broken record comment by Congresswoman Waters of; "impeach 45" was not working as she hoped, it appears she has opted for a more aggressive route to resistance. Sadly, people buy into a negative narrative, when they have been convinced by opinion bias, that President Trump, his administration, family, and supporters or voters, are misogynistic, homophobic, racist, bigoted, Nazis, fascists, and are the vile evil of the earth. When civility between parties takes a sharp turn from respect for indifference, only division, hatred, and harm will ensue. The once learned element of respect flows both ways, just like the ocean tide, a phenomenal balance in nature, we too should have that same ease of respectful existence with each other.

ANOTHER DRAMA
FILLED ELECTION

Constitutionally the time will come again for another election cycle; whether it be political midterms or presidential, all Americans need not take the vote for granted as it is ever so important, now more than any. Our country has become so divided and polarized with many who have been influenced away from the very reason why our founding fathers created this country. While those of us who are still alive with the knowledge of times gone past, we still hold within ourselves the core values of genuine American democracy. We need to vote out these politicians that no longer work for all of us, stand up to their obstructionist views, deaf ears to our cries for justice, help from the suppressions and oppressions that their blatant disregard or inappropriate actions have caused us.

The checks and balances are not to be left to the governmental agencies, committees, and political oversight organizations, but more so by the people. As we all know of or have witnessed, many of these oversight organizations are run by some of whom have been later found to be bought and paid for by lobbyists or contributors that may not hold our best interests as the people first and foremost, therefore the checks and balances must revert to the people.

Remember when you were in school, and the president was going to speak? The schools stopped their lessons as everyone quietly and respectfully listened via intercom, radio, or watched on the classroom television barely coming in unless you put excess amounts of aluminum foil on the antennas or "rabbit ears" as we called them back then.

My son began his school years right around the timeline of the implementation of "no child left behind" there arose a drastic change in the curriculum which started to steer away from the necessary foundations of learning that many of us; baby boomers and those born during the next decade after were taught. As our students learned about the history of the world, afflictions of other countries, they were now being conditioned to the thought that America must be the caregiver and savior of the rest of the world first and foremost. At that point, I knew that my son would need to learn American history at home, so out came the library books and homeschooling began in addition to what was supposed to be taught by the educational system.

Once my son entered middle school, the "common core" newly devised method of teaching was in full swing the promoted method of education being so advanced and would make our children excel at a phenomenal rate over all other educationally superior countries. This educational atrocity would change the thought patterns and societal perceptions of our children for a generation to come.

Coupled with this fantastic "common core" came "new math." Last I knew two plus two equals four, smooth and calculated within less than 2 seconds, and this is if you take your time. Now there is this seemingly multi-step process to get to the same point. No more times table charts, no more graphs for memory retention; now you must apply this ludicrous format of calculation to get to the same place. The ultimate insanity for a parent who must soon attempt to help with homework, as if algebra wasn't crazy enough, now we have a mile-long simple math problem. What brainiac came up with this one?

Many may fault the educators for the educationally lost society of millennials, Xennials, or Generation X, the followers of fork-tongued shepherds. Not all teachers are to blame, and in defense of those who genuinely wish to teach their students by old school methods in today's academic atmosphere find themselves castrated from creativity no longer able to treat each child by their strengths and weaknesses. Or those who creatively taught to understand the complicated, are forced to comply with a meticulously thought out lesson plan, good, bad, or indifferent, to the positive or many times to the negative of the student regardless.

On occasion, Speaker Nancy Pelosi was noted to be confused as to who the current president was, as if in denial or perhaps a more logical explanation of a diagnosis of elderly dementia. Once Speaker Pelosi finally acknowledged who the president-elect is, she is now forever filled with propaganda and misleading rhetoric that she presents to the American people regularly with comments that are almost as divisive as her counterpart from California Congresswoman Maxine Waters.

Congresswoman Waters has also been in office far longer than she should have. Congresswoman Waters clicks up the rhetoric, a few notches more each chance she encounters. Whether it be jumping on the Red Hen bandwagon and calling for action against conservatives, Trump supporters, cabinet and administration members, or actions against the family of our president, it was a sad day for our country when the media began highlighting this grandstanding by Waters. The social media negative posts were in full swing, all in support of Waters or against Waters' comments. Instead of realizing the potential damage, division, and hatred she was inciting by her podium propaganda, in an interview Waters pushed back at the president, blaming him for any negative feedback she encountered from her rhetoric, not acknowledging nor walking back any portion of her comments which caused the reverse negativity. What should be an obvious point that Waters was aware of what message she was sending and what may potentially happen if someone heard her intended message taking it to fuel their fire of hatred. Waters alleged that she had received death threats and began to cancel some of her appearances. I awaited the use of the "race card," which inevitably came when a group of black women in office and those within the black caucus wrote a letter on the alleged or perceived mistreatment of Maxine Waters. Regardless, the pigmentation of her skin, Waters has been consistently outspoken and divisive throughout her political career in California, only exacerbated post-2016 election where her podium grandstanding has taken a dangerously inciteful tone and should not be without condemnation, no matter the color of her skin or genealogy.

On the contrary, the president should also refrain from the "low IQ" comment when referring to Waters as it is also condescending without necessity; therefore, playing into the resistance agenda. Waters' primary talking point which makes her feel validated since President Trump entered office has been, "impeach 45", which she chants wildly along with her attendees, technically no different than those who chant, "lock her up," "build that wall," or "USA," at Trump rallies across the country. The significant difference being that Congresswoman Waters is inciting or implying violence with her comments, "make sure they know they are not welcome," "impeach 45", or "push them back," whereas comments chanted, "lock her up," are referring to the double standards of justice that people feel was given to Hillary Clinton during her email investigation, dossier from a foreign entity, DNC and Clinton Foundation improprieties. The "build that wall," refers to the southern border to secure safety for American citizens, further preventing illegal border crossings, forcing all migrants to enter the United States legally through the designated points of entry. The loudest of all heard at all Trump rallies would be, "USA," which candidate now president Trump had vowed and now stands by his word to; "Put America First," which resonates loudly with millions of Americans across the country. To the opposite, spectrum end, Trump's opposition or those select Democrat political talking heads, prefer the #ForThePeople, claim without differentiating what or whom unless the identity agenda presents itself, in the moment of resistance or office campaign speech.

Regardless of whom the president-elect is in our country, the people spoke and cried out loudly when electing president Trump into office in 2016. Those who voted were thankful that the founders of our country opted to form the 12th Amendment of the United States Constitution when it was found to be potentially problematic in an election with states holding a much larger population than others may inevitably control every election not allowing a democratic fair and balanced election. The 12th Amendment was ratified at different times during the first few years in the 1800s by each state individually utilizing the electorate process in the election of 1804.

California, on the other hand, stands by different rules of their own regarding the designation of the 55 electoral votes granted to them, which is now governed by the National Popular Vote Interstate Compact initially vetoed by Governor Schwarzenegger in 2006 and later adopted by Governor Brown in 2011.

California beats to a different drum when it comes to electing their public officials, which itself has proven problematic. What became apparent after the election of 2016 was where the Democrat elected officials began their propagandist agenda, voters were refusing to accept the electoral conclusion because Hillary Clinton led by more than 3 million California voters overall, therefore not accepting the results. The media began their forceful denial, overdramatizing the results in a doomsday appearance, further propagating violent protests and unrest. Hillary Clinton would not make her concession speech until being forcefully prompted only to portray herself in denial. Post concession speech Hillary Clinton began her national and world book tour of the "what happened" narrative blaming everyone from the FBI Director Comey to the Macedonians.

Although we may not agree with our presidents over the years, we hope that they will be the one to lift the oppressions that are experienced daily, across the board. We must remember it is not only the president that makes the decisions and puts forward actions or laws we are supposed to live by; it is our congressional elected politicians who primarily stone-wall or vote block the real changes. This 2016 election, more so than any other we as people, should realize that those who have been in office for multiple terms have now become those that work against the people in the majority. Many politicians have become detached from the reality of what the American people are experiencing, in the same thought pattern noted from Hillary Clinton, who separated from the reality of the voters and yet another reason why she lost the election. Life-long politicians like Hillary Clinton, Nancy Pelosi, Maxine Waters, and many others who have been in the political scene for decades, have been caught up with the selling of themselves at any cost to remain in power or control, saying whatever is necessary to do so. Many political heads live with security details assigned to them and their families, live in lavish homes with above-average financial means, unlike the average hardworking American.

The politicians' detachment continues when they fail to walk among their constituents outside of the auditorium campaign settings. The mere change in the psychology of the elected politician can be seen evolving over the decades. Speeches, campaign promises, interactions with others, mannerisms, and lifestyle changes, place a politician in a luxurious environment of privilege further forgetting they have stepped into power on the backs of those they now ignore who are lacking highly profitable financial capabilities or perceived social status. It is rare to find a "down to earth" politician post-election cycle.

During the 2016 election cycle, as I was beginning to research for this book each candidate had their slogan, with Hillary Clinton it was, "I'm With Her" which appeared to stick more than, "we are stronger together" with those I spoke to and Donald J Trump, "Make America Great Again." When I asked if any individual why they were "with her," either the comment was, "she is a woman," "she is for women," "I don't like Trump," rarely any other narrative. With Trumps' slogan, generally the same, people were, "tired of high taxation," "high insurance premiums under Obamacare," "jobs," "tired of everything on the shelves made in China," "welfare reform," "tired of the military overseas fighting battles where we don't belong," illegal immigration was always at the top of the list in close running with security of the nation.

Then-candidate Donald J Trump connected with the people every time he opened his mouth with his off-the-cuff style. Granted, Trump is a billionaire; however, he didn't speak nor carry himself like the average billionaire, never presented himself as above anyone nor came off as condescending to the average working class. Trump's demeanor was just like the everyday average Joe with the same concerns as everyone else who paid attention or cared about the direction the country was dangerously headed. Common sense would tell you that as a business-minded individual if the people are working, the country is prospering, so is the company, hence substantial financial gain.

Granted, during many a speech he would make targeted comments like; "Crooked Hillary," and now "Crazy Maxine," "Lying Ted," MS-13 are "animals," these were target specific not generalized as the Basket of Deplorables comment made by Hillary Clinton, toward millions of Americans because they didn't support her.

Neither candidate was perfect, both were known infidels, subject to criticism at every turn, a party to questionable interactions and business practices, subject to prior lawsuits and settlements, however only one candidate would be targeted as committing multiple atrocities known to the American voter, and that was Hillary Clinton. Not only had Hillary Clinton lied about Benghazi, but she had also been subjected to very questionable investigations over the years, many of which were looked at with the utmost criticism when parties who were set to testify against the Clintons met with an untimely demise. The Clinton Foundation ultimately scrutinized for its hypocritical donations by foreign countries that committed atrocities toward women, questionable, alleged, and confirmed failures in Haiti. Questions still surrounded the Uranium One deal with Russia and controversies abounded regarding Benghazi, during her time in office as Secretary of State under then-president Obama. Hillary Clinton took it for granted that she could dazzle or pull the wool over millions of Americans eyes as she had done for decades and learned quite well how to do, never realizing that there were millions more who were not impressed and paid attention with memories, like an elephant, to coin the phrase.

Donald J Trump was not without critique as his moralistic sexual improprieties would become the forefront and his historical Taj Mahal restructuring bankruptcy filing, which led to the financial strains or closures of many small businesses.

To this day and most likely will never come to fruition, Hillary Clinton and many of her Democrat colleagues all of whom shall never accept the outcome of the 2016 election. Hillary Clinton will continue to be in denial, never admitting it was her character and professional flaws that made her unwelcomed in the White House as the first woman president. So many people, men, and women alike specified that they would like to see a woman president, but not Hillary Clinton, many named; Condoleezza Rice, even now and after the fact candidate, would have been Ambassador to the United Nations, Nikki Haley. Granted, both women are Republicans, none the less, these named individuals came from all political viewpoints, who were basing their choices on merit alone.

CALL TO VOTE

A good quote from the former 38th president of the United States, Gerald R Ford, "A government big enough to give you everything you want is a government big enough to take from you everything you have." If you let this one sink in for a moment, we are pretty much there, wouldn't you think? A classic example would be that of Obamacare, which claimed for all but took from many, in an unconstitutionally unfair manner. Welfare subsidies, refugee resettlement funds, and financial aid to illegal aliens in our country can fall into this categorization as well. Democrat philosophies of today believe in handouts unlike ever before, without thought to consequences of the hardworking American that must cut corners or make hard financial choices to afford the additional taxation. Republicans nor any other alternative party are being held unaccountable either. We, as a nation need to make sure they hear our voices loud and clear.

Another inciteful quote is from Samuel Adams, a philosopher and founding father of our country, "If ever a time should come when vain and aspiring men shall possess the highest seats in Government, our country shall stand in need to prevent its ruin." How sadly accurate this quote is with divisive leaders of whom have been elected into office, standing on the premise of their right to free speech, propagating fear and unrest in an agenda-drive to harm the fabric of our society through divisive rhetoric.

Although, many of the obstructionist talking heads are predominantly from the states of California, New York, and unfortunately my home state of Connecticut, we the people can no longer sit idle and must do our very best to vote these men and women out of office, placing new blood in who will work for all of us. If they fail, boot them out also.

As an independent voter, I always wanted to leave my options open and never wished to tie myself into any titled political party. Generally, depending upon your opposition, if you voted for a Republican, you hated Democrats, and if you voted democrat, you hated republicans, which were to be rather moronic. Blatantly evident, the Democrat party of today plays identity politics, swaying with the wind, dependent upon the next probable event to make a politically motivated statement.

When our country experienced another high school shooting, the Democrats lobbied around teenaged, high schoolers, convincing them that they had their best interests, and if they protest or walk out of class, they will be a movement heard; the change would come, no more shootings will happen. With this new voice, the Democrats began to lobby to lower the voting age, feeling that this newly energized group of potential voters would help them regain seats in the midterm or presidential elections. Needless to cite, this attempt failed, and the protests, walkouts, and likely change fell to the wayside, although remained a talking point and lobbied agenda item. The unfortunate part of this narrative is that the protests were misled and not focused on the real issues surrounding the societal changes, lack of follow-through on the levels of the school, local and federal law enforcement agencies. The Democratic party consistently plays the 2nd Amendment game every time, never addressing the root of the problem and casts blame on an inanimate object instead of the individual and systemic failures.

The Democrats and their Republican counterparts have lacked a real message of actual change for the American people. New Era Democrats rely mostly on those indoctrinated with the common core ideologies of socialism, globalism, and identity, therefore believing if they lobby these groups by designation, they will turn out in droves to vote them in. The psychosocial political gameplay has worked for quite some time, to a point where our society has an overabundance of misled individuals who will vote on propaganda without independently thinking outside the box.

For decades the Democrat party controlled the predominantly black or minority vote, with the misconception given to them that they are the party of change. Promises consistently made on the political campaign platform to afford more abilities to this select group of individuals, where once elected, failed on their empty campaign promises and opted to provide subsidies to enable codependency instead of prosperity and progression to self-sufficiency.

Throughout the decades, the democrat party propagated half-truths that they are for the oppressed yet find comfort in suppression instead.

The Democrat Party, #ForThePeople narrative has now come into play as the new era democrat party attempts to make promises, not just for the predominantly black community, they wanted more; therefore they reach out to any group or identity considered in the societally viewed minority class of individuals, inclusive of illegal aliens. The Democrats lobby on a platform need for change branding party opponents win can only be by voter suppression, gerrymandering, and supremacy, hence the race-baiting card. The inclusivity of all people in the democrat message allows the right to vote for illegal aliens in this country, which constitutionally is not permitted. Nonetheless, in many states, such as California, illegal aliens are being allowed to vote in some local elections, setting the precedence for enhancement to other election levels.

Americans have seen the needs of the few outweigh those of many, especially in this new era of illegal immigration issues. As it has always been the general rule, if an adult commits a crime and becomes incarcerated, the minor child into the custody of another. If no family member is available to care for the minor child, they are placed by the social services agency in foster care until the adult is released and deemed competent to care for the child again. We, as a society, would think this to be commonplace and a no brainer when it comes to illegal border crossings, right? On the contrary, a majority of; Democrats in office, with only a select few on the fence of surety or those running for reelection, in conjunction with the mainstream media, have chosen a different path.

As the Trump administration looks to reform illegal crossings, the requests for legislative changes encounter obstruction by elected congressional figures. Those that lobby for illegals on their alleged constitutional right to fair legal representation once they step on U.S. soil feel that those who are not citizens of our country deserve a different set of standards. Hence, the new era democrat running platform. The narrative of babies or children separated at the border; we must save the babies and keep them with their parents at all costs is still questionable as we are not assuring that these babies or children are safely allowed to remain with their actual biological parents is a hard voter push. Now we enter the double standards of justice, an effort to obstruct, tear at the heartstrings of general populous, and another vote potential.

Even with the LGBTQ, pro-choice, and sanctuary city ideologies of societal progression, Democrats are still finding it hard to secure a real message for all voters, failing to sway them entirely for the final vote. With midterms and the next presidential election cycling again, the Democrats have seemingly opted to tap into the Bernie Sanders followers, the Millennials or Xennials, that may come out if they have younger, more progressive thinking candidates.

After the upset in the New York primaries noted to be a potential tide of change when Alexandria Ocasio-Cortez defeated Joseph Crowley, a breath of fresh air came to the new era democrat liberal platform and an element of concern for conservatives. Although this candidate is young, her ideas are not compatible with the millions who voted for the "America First" agenda in the 2016 presidential election. Not only is Alexandria Ocasio-Cortez, radically misinformed or lacking in factual data when she presents her ideas, she quickly became a notable talking piece for both liberal and conservative media outlets. To the detriment of the futuristic solvency of America, this style of new era democrat is afforded too much airtime in many countries', in the minds of her followers, she appears credible, when in fact, the contrary is true.

From Democrat Party endorsements of the younger candidate Kevin De Leon over the elder office holding Diane Feinstein, elections of Alexandria Ocasio-Cortez, Ilhan Omar, to the addition of Beto O'Rourke to the presidential candidacy platform run, the party appears to be attempting to take hold of their generationally indoctrinated children.

The Republican party is way too silent and lackluster when it comes to calling their voters to the ballot box. The pied-piper president is the voice of the party, and he must come out and campaign for them as well as maintain his duties as needed for the country. The Republican platform is relatively simple as portrayed to those who listen; they are constitutionalists, want security for the country, enhanced military, provide tax incentives, pro-jobs, pro-life, and desire immigration reform with current laws abided. It would seem simple, but not in the era of social media, opinion journalism, #resistance, and obstructionism.

I can barely remember a time when my grandparents or family didn't find their way to the ballot box and vote. My husband recalls a time when his previous in-laws were afraid not to vote, feeling it was a violation of their becoming naturalized citizens of the United States or may face deportation, which I would agree. Both my grandmothers were of the same thought pattern.

The fact is you cannot have change without voting for someone who will make a radical lobby for change independent of the strategic norm in politics. As an independent voter, I am unable to vote in the primaries due to no party affiliation, this can be positive or negative for a candidate that I may see as an excellent potential change agent. I have been disappointed in some of my picks, and perhaps should have chosen differently, but then again that is how the process works.

For example, I had always voted for our Democrat Senator Richard Blumenthal, of whom worked so well for the people of Connecticut when he was the Attorney General. I voted for him for the last time in 2016; I learned the reality of my poor choice quickly as he has become one of the most disappointing of political heads, failing to uphold the constitution by changing the interpretation to fit the needs of the resistance agenda. Additionally, he has lobbied for frivolous lawsuits against the Trump administration to thwart progress without regard that it hinders a positive effect for millions of hardworking Americans that can no longer afford or attain their American dreams. Among the illegal immigration and sanctuary city promotion, Senator Blumenthal's propaganda promoted on the most biased of media outlets, MSNBC, is only a few reasons why I and many others will never vote for him again.

Another propaganda "junkie" is our Senator Chris Murphy, who never ceases to amaze with his globalist ideologies, lobby for the circumvention of immigration laws, and high school style social media play to attract supporters. Murphy consistently attempts to undermine the office of the president, calling for obstruction or resistance at every turn. He, too, is a favorite of MSNBC and Twitter, using both platforms to promote his divisive agenda with misconceptions and hypocrisy. Much like my view of; Hillary Clinton, I have found Murphy, an advocate of being on a self-promotion platform taking credit for the achievements of others as his own. When Senator Murphy is questioned or called out on Twitter, Murphy's supporters rarely have a rebuttal to proven facts and data.

Connecticut has become, in my view, a little California, with its sanctuary cities, circumvention of laws, high taxation, and governmental ineptitude. We have courts that rule to obstruct the actions of the Department of Justice, we have questionable voting practices, high subsidies in concentrated minority areas, including but not limited to elected senators, mayors, and city officials who come out in support of illegal aliens of whom are in violation of deportation or check-in orders. We also had suffered through our Democrat Governor Malloy of whom lobbied for sanctuary cities, and illegal aliens, one of whom was in our state for 24 years, never attempted to become naturalized, was in violation of a check-in order, had four children, received subsidies, and was due to be deported for non-compliance. All actions, a direct slap in the face to those who came to this country legally and became naturalized. Before the end of his tenure, Governor Malloy signed an order to allow illegal alien DACA to take advantage of the educational funding programs which potentially disallows the legal U.S. born students to take advantage of these financial programs when funding has been exhausted and depleted. Where is the fairness in any of this?

One would think that anyone tired of paying high taxation, immigration law circumvention, financial ineptitudes, and financial misappropriations would not vote for another Democrat running on the same or similar platform, but they did. The 2018 Republican candidate for Governor of CT, Bob Stefanowski, had a clear plan to start a square one with the budget, believed in tax reform, repealing the dual taxation, legal immigration enforcement, to name a few, and lost to a Democrat candidate, Ned Lamont, who is critically termed, Malloy 2.0. Not to any surprise of those who listened, our new Democrat governor has come true to his empty promises, and we now head for more taxation, tolls, and more burdens to face as residents of CT. Many would ask or tell you, move if you do not like it. Easier said than done when you own property in a state that has high taxation, decreased property values, family obligations, businesses, and invested in a state that you lived in for your lifetime.

We as a state could not manage to break free of the democrat stronghold, as many of us hoped we could. Our new governor, Ned Lamont, campaigned on "no increase in taxes, identity politics, fear-mongering healthcare platform. To his credit, this has proven technically correct. However, he may have stated no increase; he did not say any new taxes. In pure Democrat form, one of his first proposals in office was to tax groceries and medications, which in turn would further financially affect those he claimed to be an advocate. These two human necessities for survival now must come at a higher cost to the already poverty-stricken, the sick, and the elderly. This announcement did not come without considerable backlash, which falls on deaf ears.

It cannot be stressed enough that we all need to get out and vote and remain diligent to voting improprieties, to hold on to our country, its constitutional rights, and the very platform that our founding fathers wanted for us. It is fascinating to think that over two centuries ago, our founders had the foresight to realize that one day, we could be faced with the choice or need to take a strong stand against the government once rightfully elected as our vote no longer matters in the democracy intended. We are in the crossroad where our government has failed us, becoming too independent of the people no longer representing all Americans fairly. We have witnessed a polarization between the parties, one trying to uphold the will of the people through adherence to the constitution and the other through fear, misguidance, and propagandist division, to circumvent or rewrite the constitution. Millions came together voted in a real change agent, a shaker and mover, named Donald J Trump. He cannot do it alone; it will be dependent upon, we the people, to place our beautiful country back on the tracks of progress with respect for our past and uphold our constitution.

We all have a new battle to engage within our own country, which is divisiveness propagated by these new era democrats who hypocritically lobby against what they advocated for in the past only because they have a non-conformist in the White House. Along with the media play, we have a generation of young voters who have a new thought pattern that is not aware of a plan built upon the foundation of our country's planned freedom for its people. The past generation and a half have been led to believe we are the caregivers of the world; all are privy to our wealth and prosperity as we have a surmountable amount of wealth that we can afford all. A presumption of thought, we as a nation are perfect within our own eyes, and all other countries are considered subordinates that cannot manage without our leadership and examples set. This current generation of American youth are now maliciously utilized as a political propaganda tool, misled down a path they believe is fact, yet it is inaccurate, unknowing that those that lead them have no intention to protect them after their vote.

We cannot lose hope regardless of the obstacles that are before us. As I specify, time and again, we all must remain diligent, calling out the hypocrisies of our elected legislators. We are drained, tired, and worn from working to hold on to the fruits of our labors, however, we cannot sleep as we are in a crucial point in our soon to be history. Watch every candidate, every ballot, voter roster, every voter, be diligent to the validity of our elections for it is not just by foreign propaganda that sways opinion or casts each vote but by improprieties proven in our elections found after the fact due to human error or intervention.

My view is not different from millions of Americans in this country; however, we are labeled conspiracy theorists when the contrary is true. We all have thought it once or twice that our vote matters not, so why bother as the election was already chosen in advance, right? We cannot allow these thoughts to influence us any longer. As the farmers and countrymen came out of the fields to battle the British, we now must come out of our homes and make our voices heard to save our country from what is on a far-left, globalist, social dependency political track to either a dictatorship government or socialist regime that will inevitably destroy us.

SLIM PICKINS'

With a new presidential election cycle in the future, 2020 set to be comic relief, rollercoaster ride, or field of lunacy. As the bushel is overflowing with many sour apples representing the democrat party choices, we must remind ourselves of the 2016 election and the underhanded tactics that pushed Hillary Clinton to the forefront, becoming the chosen one to lead the candidacy in 2016. Not only did we see and hear a pure condescension for the American people, but we also viewed a high level of hypocrisy. After the democrat loss in 2016, we have been inundated with a false casting of blame, fabricated accusations, costly investigations, divisive platform rhetoric like never before. We have witnessed the contradictions of a democrat party claiming to be #ForThePeople while casting disgust, ridicule, or insult to the intelligence of the people by that same party. It is now the same party which I have referenced as the "new era democrats" who seek to destroy our country. "PAY ATTENTION PEOPLE," think outside the box, ask yourselves, why does the democrat party lobby for illegal aliens, lowering the voting age to 16, or stand against the citizenship question on the census form? In case anyone forgot, the rest of this chapter shall serve as a small reminder.

In 2016 on the Democrat side, there was an interestingly strong candidate named; Bernie Sanders from New Hampshire who most definitely swayed on a different swing than his democrat associates, running as a socialist-style candidate. His message was firm, durable, and what many wished to hear such as; free education, take down the lobbyists, wall street was the root of evil, free healthcare for all now platform titled "Medicare For All," and many a time knocking the rhetoric preached by the oppositions. His base was primarily younger voters, college-aged with so many hopes for themselves, but still unsure of their next leap without the safety net of mom and dad. These "Bernie" supporters would later be labeled, "basement dwellers," by the same candidate who labeled the Trump supporters, "deplorables."

The Democrats had their golden girl, the breaker of the glass ceiling, Hillary Clinton, of whom would prove to be quite the candidate not much different than the candidate of 2008, who ran against Barack Obama. Hillary Clinton would run on a message of change, without a clear message, without modification to the status quo, implying it but never stating precisely what she was running on. Hillary Clinton did have the experience of Washington, knew the in's and out of politics, and was "well connected." Out of 6 original democrat candidates, these two would remain the strongest with many twists and turns to come.

As rallies began to gain more attendees for Bernie Sanders, it seemed as though this could be the Democrat candidate that would lead the party. His crowds were astounding, mimicking a lesser version or those of candidate Trump. Granted, if I were still back in college knowing that my surmounting student loan debt could be paid off, nonexistent, and if I were ignorant to the facts of how government appropriations work, I would have been on board too. His messages were all delivered with a concerned face, pointing the finger and shouted determination to get his point across. He presented himself as that sweet, but scowl faced grandpa, scolding you but not really.

Hillary Clinton was in a league all her own. When I was in college, I opted to write a paper on powerful women in my lifetime, concentrating on then-First Lady Hillary Rodham Clinton. My research took me back to researchable documentation of her reported childhood, college aspirations, law studies, courtship to Bill, work as a prosecutor, First Lady of Arkansas to her position, then First Lady of the United States of America. It was during this research that I became enlightened, especially with her persecution of a young child who had been abused and brutally raped. This case proved an unfortunate and disturbing reading.

In 2008, when Hillary Clinton began her run against Barrack Obama, it was my research coupled with many long years of observations, that prevented me from even considering her. Many of the political comments and mudslinging that was done by then-candidate Obama was, in general, true and learned to be fact. I had always never thought of her as a victim when it came to then-President Bill Clinton's infidelities and inappropriate actions toward women, I found myself thinking the same, "if she cannot manage her own house, how can she manage the White House?". Not for granted, infidelity has many causes and two parties to allow it. Thankfully she was not the "chosen one" in 2008, and it appeared it was the time of the first black president. Therefore, Barrack Hussein Obama was elected and for two consecutive terms.

The Republicans started with 17 candidates on stage, what a line up it was. Jeb Bush who wished to become yet another Bush in the family of presidents, only to drop out early, literally with his tail between his legs. Ben Carson, a non-political head, a black man who came from simple means working his way up to becoming a highly respected surgeon, well versed, and on the top of my list of favorites. Ted Cruz, a senator from Texas, who was also a top runner, had a consistent message for the country. Ted Cruz's mannerisms and way of speaking reminded me of Richard Nixon, though. Senator Cruz would later choose another Republican contender as his female running mate, Carly Fiorina. Through all the mud-slinging, name-calling, debating, the final two candidates standing were amazingly John Kasich, Governor of Ohio, and Donald J Trump, New York businessman. The sheer curiosity of this election was fascinating.

Oddly enough and coincidental, my son and I traveled to New Hampshire one afternoon to make an equipment delivery, later stopping for lunch in Manchester at the Pie Company, we found ourselves part of an exciting and memorable event. While we were eating a large bus pulled up outside and in walked, Republican candidate, Governor John Kasich with his entourage in tow. The staff of the business cleared out the back area where we were seated, leaving us and another couple, putting numerous tables together, and they all sat down for some amazingly great pizza. If you are ever in Manchester, New Hampshire most definitely check them out, and no, they didn't pay me to write that.

After my son and I finished our lunch, we exchanged a few words with Governor Kasich and a couple of his staffers. I wished him luck in the primaries, and with a mouth full of food, he graciously said, "thank you." Although somewhat insignificant, it was a helpful interaction for my son as a new voter. I wondered if this could be our next president, but it didn't seem so. You know how you get that gut feeling; it just wasn't there, unless it was because we overate, and there was no more room for emotion. I did know that Governor Kasich was one of the few governors who kept their state in the black. Even with the high costs of healthcare subsidies, he maintained jobs growth and a balanced budget with a surplus. I thought to myself that if then-Governor Kasich was able to manage and do this, perhaps, he has a chance. Ultimately to his deficit, he did not have a clear and concise message even though he was one of the few left standing at the podium.

Not too many candidates passed through our state of Connecticut as we are a smaller state and perhaps not one of electorate importance to many; however, we did see Hillary Clinton, Bernie Sanders, and Donald J Trump. All three with campaign rallies that would be well remembered for many, including ourselves.

Candidate Hillary Clintons' rallies were not as massive as either Bernie Sanders nor Donald Trumps' but not lacking in excitement and mudslinging. She spoke of the woman's movement, rights, equal pay, how she wanted freedoms, how excellent the healthcare was, and that she was proud to have been a part of it. She spoke of how she wanted an influx of refugees to flee the tyranny in their countries and come to the United States for a better life, and how she was an advocate for progress and change. Her message was with no real change to those who were looking forward to the possibility of the first female president. Although, Hillary Clinton had the "I'm with her" following, many who had followed the Clintons and remembered the actions of Secretary of State Hillary Clinton under President Obama, were not as easily convinced that she was the right choice for the country, first woman, breaker of the glass ceiling or not.

Bernie Sanders had a great show of supporters at his rally's, and as I mentioned before, many were college-aged and some who were not too comfortable with Hillary Clinton. You could see those who attended hung on every word, this silver-haired, determined speaker would utter, such as free tuition for all, regulate Wall Street, take power away from the big banks. No different a candidate than as to today, with his finger pointing to make his words evident as he stated the same from rally to rally, but never mentioned one primary fact to his narrative, how. He was consistent in his determination on his view as to what was wrong with America, and on many concerning points he was on target, but never how he was going to accomplish it, nonetheless, those who knew little of the struggles past the comforts and stabilities of the nest, he was their new comfort zone. He did seem like he was going to beat out Hillary in the primaries, especially with the voter support, and following that Sanders had, it was utterly unbelievable that he didn't become the Democrat candidate, but then again there was the DNC and Hillary Clinton.

Up until the Trump rally held on April 15th in Connecticut, we were leaning toward Bernie Sanders, not without extreme reservations though, as Bernie Sanders was preaching socialism in a severe form, which I knew would not work for the betterment of the country. Here we go again with the gut feeling, which was telling me to keep listening to what everyone else had to preach about, counting on another potential or better choice. Well, at least I was praying for one.

Now we will address the turning point for me, my family, and millions of others across the country, Donald J Trump, his message, and his rallies. My son, Nicholas, now able to vote, was far more attentive to the election process. My husband, Gary, was just as tuned in, more so than any other presidential election in the past. At times I wondered if it was the drama of it all or absolute concern of where our country was and how pivotal this election would be this year. I most definitely knew that the voting choice would be so crucial for all of us, and in my heart that we as a country would not be able to survive any further free for all or globalist thinking president.

Generally, local, state and national elections are all the same and follow the same path of rhetoric spewing, promise-filled election speeches, most of which rarely come to fruition. Another "file 13" season with the seemingly never-ending political postcards, flyers, and propaganda adds that took up more time during your favorite TV show than the repetitive commercials: more items to be shredded, more flipping of the channels. So many trees killed and so much time wasted.

I thought to myself what an experience it would be to attend a campaign rally with my son, so I signed onto the FOX61 website and signed up for three tickets to participate in the rally coming to Hartford, CT on April 15th, 2016. My husband wasn't too excited because he hates large crowds, but still went and now speaks of his experience regularly. So, I guess this is one of those, "honey, I told you so moments."

The plan was to make this a family event. However, when I tried to print the tickets, I was unable to. I ended up sending a quick email to the FOX61 news station explaining the print issue and received not only an email response but a phone call from Virginia Fisher, who was the current producer of FOX61. A phone call that would change quite a bit for all of us in the days and months to come.

At first, I thought that this was a call from yet another bogus solicitor or google robocall, but I answered anyway. Of course, answering in a pissy, stern voice expecting to either be hung up on, told I need a security system, new roof, won a cruise, or help someone with drug rehab or perhaps my google listing was expired. Now I'm sure many of us get these calls and hate them terribly. Nope, none of the above, to my surprise, the caller was human. After explaining my tone of voice, Virginia laughed and completely understood, I told of the print out glitch, and we did get it straightened out. After a couple of moments, she began to ask me my political views and those of my family, after hearing my opinionated views on everyday issues, Virginia asked if we would be willing to head to the news station for a quick interview with Jenn Bernstein, one of the local station reporters before the rally. I reluctantly agreed to go to the news station because I knew how ridiculous it is to get around in Hartford and wanted to be sure we would have enough time to get to the rally. Virginia assured me that we would be out in time. Then I let my son and reluctant husband know, our plans had changed a bit.

After getting lost and meandering around downtown Hartford a few times circling the same block, we found our way to the security entrance of the station, parked, then signed in with the guard. We were directed to the elevator and rode our way up to the station floor where the elevator doors opened, where stood before us a tiny petite woman in very high heels, that barely made her any less delicate. After introducing herself as Jenn Bernstein, whom we all knew from seeing her on the television, however, she appeared much taller on screen. Then we were greeted by Virginia Fisher, the station producer. It was interesting that they were waiting for us as the elevator doors opened, we wondered to ourselves whether they were making sure we seemed reasonable or credible enough to put on the air for an interview, and if not, in what manner would they shoo us away if we seemed or looked a bit too crazy. I guess we passed the test. The two women escorted us to the set where my son Nicholas and I would be answering whatever questions they may throw at us. My husband, Gary, although curious about the entire station, was not interested in the 10-minute limelight event, however anxious to meet Rachel Franks, our local weather girl.

As the media crew set us up with our microphones and began a sound test, they realized that my son was 6'2" and towered over both Jenn and me, so we were conveniently given boxes to stand on, convenient and revealing. At that point, we all knew why such a petite woman could be as tall as her counterpart Lorenzo Hall of whom was much taller than my son when we met Lorenzo Hall later during our departure. After the sound bites were in, we were ready for action. Granted, both of us were a bit nervous, however, managed through the process of conveying why we were there in Hartford that evening. We were asked the general question of; why we were heading to the rally, what we hoped to gain from it, and a brief take on our views. Our few minutes of fame were through, down the elevator, and out the door, we went. We hurried to the car and headed to find parking further downtown. Little did we know this would not be our last interview that we would have with FOX61. We were called back for follow up discussions and rebuttals a couple more times as the political race progressed.

Our 10 minutes of fame over our printout tickets in hand, we headed to the line that was already forming at the entrance doors of the convention center. We encountered people and crowds that had already been gathering, which encompassed supporters, those out of curiosity, protesters, vendors, and those that were seemingly, just there. And by, just there, I mean just there, nothing better to do.

We did manage to get there early enough, so we were towards the front of the line. The wait wasn't too long before security opened the doors, and we all began to file in, presenting our tickets, and processed through the metal detectors. After being directed up the escalators then headed toward tables with preprinted signs to carry that stated; "make America great again" and "silent majority." Both terms would be the baseline statements of the Trump campaign and the two turning point statements in the months to come

After we grabbed our signs from the multiple piles on the tables, we headed into the hall where the rally was being held the first noticeable section was in the middle of the room where numerous tables were lined up, set near a stage that contained a wide variety of media cameras and news commentators. All curious attendees gathered before a stage to the front where a podium stood, then the waiting began. The music and conversation with those around us made the 3-hour wait pass by relatively quick. As we scanned the room looking for people, we knew we had many opportunities to chat with other people there. Some were supporters of change; some came just out of curiosity, some were Bernie Sanders supporters and were weighing their options, others complained mostly about how bad our state was and how disappointed with the government they were. Not one in our immediate surroundings cared too much for Hillary Clinton as our next president. There were people of all ages in attendance, and as the time went on, you could barely see the entry doors that we came into earlier because there were so many people standing behind and all around us. As the music played, people sang, danced, and got to know each other, sharing their personal political opinions and desires or hopes for the future not only with our state of Connecticut but the entire country. We began speaking to other small business owners from our state who were hoping for some favorable tax and regulatory change, as our state was being run terribly by our current governor, Dannel Malloy. Overall everyone was exhausted by being strapped financially due to the overabundance of tax regulations, EPA restrictions, healthcare fiascos, and immigration issues facing all of us.

There was a woman, I would say in her mid to late 50s who approached my husband and asked if she could lean against the stanchion pole that he was near. She had an obvious gimp and he was gracious to do so. She spoke understandable but broken English and told us she was there for Trump. She was a Hispanic immigrant who had emigrated to the United States, became naturalized, and settled in Connecticut. She was distraught with the lack of immigration enforcement and was 100% for the wall that Donald Trump said he wanted to build. She was very vocal about illegal immigration and bothered by the lack of enforcement. Her exact statement to us was how "the illegals are making her life hell." She elaborated on how jobs were hard to get; she paid so much money to come to the U.S., and "those people get it for free and don't become a citizen." She also went on to tell us about one of the first jobs that she had when she came here, which was as a shuttle van driver for voters. Because she spoke fluent Spanish and broken but understandable English, she was tasked to pick up people and bring them to the polls to vote. She elaborated by saying, "it was for that man Obama." She said she quit after she witnessed people who had no identification on them but still voted, and when it was time to vote for president, the person taking the ballot pointed to where and who to vote for. She was outraged and disgusted. She conveyed to us that her hopes were the same as many like her, "this businessman from New York would make leaps and bounds of change to the country because he is not a political." What we got from her was that she was tired of the politicians, and so were we and many others in attendance.

One thing we all observed before that day was that Trump was not your usual politician; he wasn't a politician at all. Most of us were quite thankful for this factor, which in part, made him a huge positive. Not only was Trump not a politician, he was not what everyone hated about politicians but learned to adapt to; politically correct. He shot from the hip, and words spilled out with no PC filter. Candidate Trump was just like everyone there; he did not speak down to us, he said it as it was, and if it is wrong or horrible, he said so, with no sugar coating. Crazy as it sounds, in the midst, of thousands, it was as if we all were just seated around the table after Sunday dinner, "shooting the breeze."

With the media reporting, we all heard the same things about this unusual candidate and their negative predictions on his ability to win the presidential race. If these predictions were so valid and noteworthy, why were so many turning out to hear him speak? Not only did then-candidate Trump want to enhance and lock down our southern border with a great big wall, but he also wanted comprehensive immigration reform with the enforcement of the laws already in place. He wanted the illegal immigrants who committed crimes to be found, incarcerated, turned over to ICE, and subsequently deported, never to come back. His primary focus would be on gangs like MS-13, and violent criminals that are filtering through our borders in record numbers, many of whom he noted were rapists and a danger to all of us. This paragraph and its contents would inevitably be used against candidate Trump not only by his opponents but the media as he would be misquoted and reported inaccurately stating "all" immigrants from Mexico were rapists and murderers, which was not right to his speech at all and millions of us heard the same address over and over, time and again. This media play on words and propaganda by opposition presidential candidates would propagate fear, thoughts of racism, the accusation of white supremacy and division amongst the nation without necessity.

No holds barred, candidate Trump took the opportunity to take a digger at our then-governor Malloy, of whom many of us were very unhappy with, so of course, there were numerous cheers and chants. We heard about the current healthcare fiasco known as the ACA or Obamacare. For many of us were proven to be unaffordable to the point that many of us no longer had healthcare because of the high premiums and deductibles. Of course, Hillary Clinton was beginning to be futuristically viewed as the potential adversary or a stronger opponent than Bernie Sanders. Therefore, candidate Trump hit the sweet spot of what millions were outraged and sensitive about, that being her email controversy and the ever so disheartening Benghazi event. Whenever Hillary Clinton's name was mentioned, the crowd chanted, "lock her up." So many saw the double standard of justice and the foul play with her alleged investigation and sweeping of facts under the rug.

Intermittently, candidate Trump would target the media, pointing at them and reiterating the unfairness of their reporting. At one point and amusingly enough the crowd turned, shaking their signs toward the stage holding the reporters and camera crew shouting; "lock them up" or "trump, trump, trump," which was a signal that there was a protester in the crowd, at which point the security or police were to escort them from the area. Anyone who followed Donald J Trump over the years knew he had a love-hate relationship with the press already, and one that would strain even more to the negative as time moved on.

On many occasions and throughout the 2016 presidential race, protesters were reported as many versus a few, and violent attacks propagated as something that wasn't. Only those in attendance were those who knew the actual reality speaking out on social media to disprove the negative rhetoric. Oddly, enough this unfair media coverage was blatantly accurate and had been significantly publicized. It was factually and purposefully misreported that protesters at the rallies were brutalized and forcefully removed. Although I cannot speak for any other gathering other than this one, the forceful removal of a protestor was not the case at all. Before the start of the rally or speech by candidate Trump, a staffer came out and instructed the attendees not to engage any protester, instead use their signs to show law enforcement the protestor location and chant repeatedly until that protester was officially escorted out of the arena. Which happened in three separate instances; each of these individuals peacefully escorted with no incident.

One of the protesters at the Hartford, CT rally, was a young girl in her mid-twenties, who laughed and cheered herself as she was escorted out. Which made us wonder why and did she even know what she was protesting? Much like some of the alleged protesters who gathered outside the entrance of the convention center with signs that stated, "stop the war." We asked ourselves, what war are they protesting? It became quite clear as time went on how disconnected people were from the current events of the day as well as how detached from the people career politicians had become. I asked one protester if they knew that Obama was president? With a cockeyed look, I further reiterated that the current president is who they should be protesting along with members of Congress of whom are in charge, not a candidate running for office. Obviously, by the glossy-eyed return stare, it was a moot point to the clueless.

With the rally coming to an end, and candidate Trump escorted off the stage out of the hall, we attendees were funneled toward the glass doors leading to an outside stairway, not directed to exit through the main entrance that we had initially entered. Stepping over the multiple pieces of ephemera, cups, and balloons left behind by others, we made our way as if in a cattle drive through these doors leading to what was designated as our exit location. As the outside doors opened and we cascaded slowly down the outdoor stairwell, we were conveniently walking through loudly, chanting protesters, angrily swearing at us all, assembled on either side of the stairway. It was uneasy and slightly intimidating. I began to wonder if this was a ploy to incite violence, and we were all being placed into a potentially hazardous situation. As we descended, some people were being spat on; water was being thrown at us, paper balls and other miscellaneous objects tossed into the crowd. As a group active against this protest display, we in the crowd began to sing the national anthem, while others chanted, "TRUMP, TRUMP, TRUMP" or "USA, USA, USA," repeatedly. I wanted to take in every bit of this moment, so I began to hold my cellphone above my head, set to record as much as I could and try to capture every element of this moment in time. To this day, the unity of those who had exited the convention center, singing our national anthem proudly, in the midst, of such angry criticism still gives me an overwhelming feeling of pride, smile, goosebumps, and tears to my eyes.

There were so many people disgracing the American flag by stomping on it, tearing it to shreds, which angered so many, my family included. One most serial moment was when this young man, I would say in his early to mid-20s, jumped off the stairway, grabbed a flag from a protester who was attempting to set it on fire. This young man was lifted by other supporters, allowing him to walk across their shoulders to stand at the corner of the building. This young man commenced to waving that American flag as I recollect and write about this young man, it still brings a massive smile to my face and an element of pride. Although, flag burning has been a commonplace protest, however, considered to be a peaceful display unlike what we are experiencing in today's environment, where it has become a method of incitement to violence. I, as well as millions of others across our nation, feel pain within our hearts and souls when someone chooses to desecrate this symbol of our freedom, country, and those who fought, still fight, and died for its historical meaning.

Even though it was like twisting their arms, both my son and husband were just as fascinated as I was with the amount of energy that filled the room and further spilled out the exit doors to the parking garage. Granted, I did empathize with them, as back in the day when I worked as an EMT, Hartford wasn't one of my favorite places to be. We all preferred the peaceful seclusion comfort back home, so it was a feat getting them to go even though they did ultimately enjoy it and continue to reflect on today. I told them to look at it as an adventure, but it turned out to be an experience we may never have again. This one experience became a candidate choice turning point for all 3 of us and many millions of others as well. We became convinced this was our choice for the next President of the United States. Little did we know what the following months leading up to the election would be like, nor the presidency yet to come.

The events of the 2016 presidential election should serve as a reminder as we head into the 2020 presidential election, where the stage is aligned with the similar yet different Democrats vying for that coveted DNC nomination. Bernie Sanders hit the trail once again, with his masterful finger-pointing, only to suffer a cardiac event casting doubt. Elizabeth Warren, claiming to be fair-minded, against Wall Street, corruption, yet falls to the side of hypocrisy, and identity improprieties herself. Then we have former Vice President; Joe Biden, who has been in the office pretty much my entire adult life, has had proven irregularities while in office, shows evident age-related deficiencies while on the campaign trail, or during lengthy debates. Beto O'Rourke has proven to be way too far to the extreme with his ideologies of 2nd Amendment suppression and governmental control. Both Kamala Harris and Cory Booker, concentrate significantly on race and identity politics, attempting to convince the potential voter that we are in a time predating Martin Luther King or the 14th Amendment. To keep the mix eclectic, we have Marianne Williamson, author, counselor to the stars, independent thinker aside from real politics and law. Although against the grain, Williamson made some interesting remarks that all Democrats on the stage should take note of; "they were not real Democrats," "she did not see one." The most moderate is; Amy Klobuchar, of whom makes a great argument and sense, yet is not to be the chosen one by the selective DNC insiders. Among others, we see Mayor Pete Buttigieg, the only gay candidate of whom America would have to be ready for a First Mister, as opposition to First Lady, if he were elected to office. Would the question be conservative America prepared for this change?

All have proven hypocrisies, promises of freebies, immigration circumvention, worldly wishes, and superiority complexes. It is a clear message to the American people that neither of these candidates will work for them first and foremost as a priority, although the claim is stated open and empty. When the Trump administration record is placed before them, they all cannot supersede nor condemn it.

Although this tossed hat of bingo balls, only one has already been chosen to run against the peoples' choice; Donald J Trump, in 2020. It is not by the vote, nor the will of the people, it is by agenda. It has been apparent and propagated as truth that the chosen one this time around maybe Joe Biden, as he is the most likely of candidates to appeal to the old-style Democrat voter.

Of course, the queen of denial, Hillary Clinton, has popped her head back into the limelight, with a giddy hint of running for president again. As the saying goes, "three strikes you're out," however, I doubt even with another strike, she would fade away or accept the outcome regardless.

As the Democrat candidate stage would dwindle to the chosen one, it would fast become apparent to the American people the choice was made long before the debate stage was set. Even with the high number of "fubars" and "misgivings," Joe Biden was the favorite. This favorite became quite apparent with the inevitable Democrat House Impeachment of our dually elected President Donald John Trump. Not only would the Democrats fail to prove their case to the American people, they further alienated millions with their railroading tactics and hypocrisies once again. Millions are left to question if the Democrat Party once for the people now a New Era Democrat Party for themselves are genuinely fighting for America's democracy, or are they just filled with malicious intent?

The people of this great nation of ours stood up, came out, and spoke loudly in 2016 by voting for Donald J Trump, and now they must scream louder, bring their neighbors, stand longer in line, and be stronger as 2020 is to be a choice between ideologies, solvency, justice, liberty, and more than just another four years.

EVERYDAY REALITY

What fast became evident and that I did know all around me, I heard stories of concern, despair, and I don't know what to do next, questions from so many concerned Americans. So many people in our State of Connecticut were out of jobs, unsure about healthcare options, business closings, corporate downsizing, and those we had known for years were leaving the state to go south or anywhere but here, hoping to find greener less costly grass to mow and an easier way to survive or retire. I always asked myself, "is it just our state, or are others just as messed up?" Well, many were in the same predicament with some variations.

A couple of acquaintances of ours decided to move to Arizona with family; both of their sons were old enough and felt it was time to put the house up for sale, sit back, and take it more manageable. Unfortunately, for them, the relocation state would prove not to be the best choice either. They both needed to maintain full-time jobs to afford what was claimed to be the "ACA" or affordable healthcare; their new chosen state would find to be one of the highest, taxpayer increases up to a reported increase of 116%. With their old house on the market, property taxes still on the rise in Connecticut and which at the time I began writing this book, Connecticut had no operating budget, and our fine Governor Malloy was threatening to institute an executive order which would deplete the municipalities of much-needed aid, forcing another tax increase on the already outlandish cost to own property in the state. To add insult to injury, our friends were still paying a small mortgage and taxes on an inherited property that was due to close, and the deal fell through.

Many would say they were stupid, didn't think ahead, should have planned better, or should have waited longer. Some would condemn the choice and leap of faith. However, I think they should be supported for their decision and wish them all the best in the world. Their story is not unlike many people from our state, and my reasoning for this example is not to a partisan model; however, it presents a viewpoint that the appearance is as though any state under democrat rule does have a problem with solvency and high tax burdens for the residents. These dual taxation states are those with predominant, financially tricky issues.

The 2016 presidential election year would show how so many people were feeling the strain of poor policies and financial ineptitudes of our 50 state and governmental oversight along with the societal burdens followed by double standards preached by manipulation. Even though our current Connecticut Governor in the 2016 election year, Dannel Malloy, thought himself to be a great Governor, claiming Connecticut is only suffering failures due to problems of the past. A politician's typical blame game, it was the fault of their predecessor, which sometimes is accurate; however, how long does it take to make a turnaround? This political blame game would be exciting to experience as Connecticut did not learn its lesson from the fiscal ineptitudes of Dannel Malloy and opted to elect another democrat governor, Ned Lamont. Ned Lamont preached change behind a campaign podium of "no more taxes," when factually shortly after his inauguration began down a path of new taxation, decreased municipal funding, a push for the creation of tolls in the state, further increasing the burdens on the taxpayers of Connecticut. With Ned Lamont's promises of no increased taxes, his play on words led to his announcements to propose a new tax on groceries and medications, which will affect everyone negatively. There is no change to our state sanctuary city policies, no hope for less funding to be cut from municipalities, no sunshine breaking through the clouds. The question to ask would be, "who shall Lamont blame, Malloy?".

Ned Lamont is still being watched closely by his election opponent, Bob Stefanowski, as well as many of us across the state. The state needed a dramatic turnaround, and at the time I wrote this book Connecticut had a reported 3,388 recorded homeless, a foreclosure rate of 2.08%, 125,000 households paying more than 50% of their income on housing, 9.6% poverty rate, 20.0% of working families under 200% of the estimated poverty line, 6.0% in extreme poverty, 4,119 children in foster care, 7.1% seniors in poverty, 10.6% persons in overall poverty, 12.6% of children in poverty, just short of a million people receiving some form of subsidy whether it be CHIP, WIC, housing assistance, food assistance, or are on full welfare benefits. As of 2017, Connecticut had an estimated population of 3.5 million people, with the reported and calculated rate of poverty and subsidies paid out we have approximately 1/3 of our state impoverished, and we are supposed to be considered a wealthy state, that thought itself is rich with fools' gold.

New York, another democrat run state, is not far off from Connecticut with a 2015-2016 poverty rate of 19.5% falling slightly from 19.9% and an overall poverty rate of 43.5% falling slightly from 44.2%. California, another democrat run state, is pushing the 19% poverty rate as well. The US is pushing close to 100 million people living in or at the poverty level; this is a 1/3 of our country's population, and the elected politicians obstruct and resist everything our president-elect, Donald J Trump tries to do to relieve the burden. Instead, many politicians go above and beyond to lobby for overseas military support, foreign aid, refugee resettlements to the United States, support and funding for illegal aliens in our country, turning a blind eye to the very facts that the people of the United States are debilitated and cannot stand for more.

The Republican-run states do not miss this criticism. However, those with a majority Democrat state legislature show a seemingly more fiscal deficit by the constituency. The rule of the democrat is taxation, taxation, taxation; this is how you bail out of insolvency, however with no jobs, lack of monetary gain, high subsidies, the additional tax is moot.

Just like the poor judgment calls for the State of Connecticut, the outgoing presidential administration under Democrat President Barack Obama was riddled with the same. What was fascinating as time went on and then-candidate Hillary Clinton was chosen as the democrat to run against the Republican candidate Donald J Trump, our governor Malloy traveled to DC to speak on his successes with our state, how fantastic a job he had done and had high hopes of being chosen as a member of Hillary Clintons administration whether coincidence or not, Governor Malloy purchased property in Maryland, closer to DC and announced that he would not be running for reelection. Thankfully for Connecticut, but not really, as if Dannel Malloy were in charge of anything, his ineptitude would follow. As fate would have it, Governor Malloy's dream didn't come to fruition.

One would ask why such decisions are made before you know who would be elected the next President of the United States? If only they could have seen into a crystal ball, they would not have been so surprised today. As a voter, would you not question this considering an election should not be cast in stone until it's over, right? I found it hard to believe America would choose another democrat that was going to run on Obama's policies when we had so many problems and the most significant deficit in history. As I mentioned before, it's all about the blame game, and the blame was on Bush, even though he had 9/11, a middle east war, and had been out of the office for eight years. Even now, as Trump is our current president, he blames Obama for much of the problems he must undertake today, some blame rightfully so, however, what was and is fast to learn for a president-elect is that many others around him make or control the decisions and directions taken. The president may make executive orders, which can be challenged and overturned. The president may put forth budget proposals, requests, and issue orders. However, dependent upon the majority party vote and votes needed exclusively for passage, all actions can be held up, thwarted, or declined.

Without being biased, the ineptitudes of the past few presidents, post-Reagan, have shown such a high element of weakness and acted not in the overall best interests of the American people. There has been so much in the way of governmental subsidies, enabling those who can work, refuse to work, or make more money under the table and collect welfare benefits that it has become a more natural way out of hard labor.

Our governmental leaders sought to enable globally, by providing aid, military protection, and settlement programs without the thought of how it would affect the everyday taxpayer and the financial burdens it puts upon them. In all actuality, life in America has become a struggle, emotionally, financially, and physically for millions. Americas once afforded opportunities have become no longer for her citizens but gifts to the world stage and those who seek to take advantage of our generosity given freely by the elites in government without a second thought to those who must endure.

Whether you reside in the State of Connecticut or across the nation, the reality is, your freedoms and liberties are being trickled away, and your daily life is now dictated to you, not by viewpoint but by everyday existence.

Facts remain, and those that millions of Americans can attest to, we need to care for ourselves and our own before all others and become a solvent country once again. Once we have done so, we shall be able to afford others. The very fact that our long term elected legislators and newly elected first-year legislators fail to see that 1/3 or more of the country of whom voted to put them in the office to care for and pass legislation to benefit are in poverty, and this is concerning. Many politicians lobby and promote the new era democrat socialist agenda, with a free for all ideology further shows a dangerous disconnect from these very democrats, when recent history surrounding the failed ACA has proven less than functional nor fiscally solvent.

We are at an impasse not only in our government but in our society as well. Fear is at the nucleus of the division, and it is the division propagated by fear from those sworn to protect the country and the people, that will make destructive desperation the victor.

My concern is no different from millions of others in the United States, where we as a country are fast approaching a civil war within our society with that between the left and right extremes of thought. There appears to be no end in sight for the propagandist media play and divisive rhetoric from many of those on the new era democrat liberal left. Even those in office for multiple years or multi-decade terms have moved to the left tipping point on the fence to capture the enabling vote with hollow promises and against the solvency of the country.

ANATOMY OF A TRUMP SUPPORTER

According to the MSM, Twitter and Facebook postings by consensus is ALL of those who support Trump are undoubtedly misogynistic, bigoted, racist, uneducated, violent, mentally unstable, stupid, foolish, hypocritical, against anyone who doesn't come from this country, hates Mexicans, fears Muslims, are supremacist, despises blacks and oddly enough allegedly hate themselves that is why they are the way they are. Although that was a mouthful, it came to hold as candidate Trump became President Trump. Some have even accused Trump supporters as being alien and not from another country; I mean outer space or another planet. It goes without explanation that much of the criticism was and still is propagated by Hillary Clinton along with her Democrat counterparts today.

You may find many hate groups that for decades even centuries, have carried down the prejudices of long ago, the majority baseline of those who voted against the status quo government and opted to roll the dice on a non-political head named; Donald J Trump wanted more substantive change far from the innate prejudices of a segregated society. Those who demanded change, wanted respect for their country, flag, military, laws, and each other, something that has been missing for so very long. The messaging terminology of; "Make America Great Again," became a chant of desire and unity with the opposition claiming division and hate. Hypocritically segregated by Democrats and their staunch followers, the use of; "Make America Great Again" was offensive and viewed as the cattle call to racism or bigotry. The hypocrisy by the Democrats is that multiple previously elected presidents have utilized this terminology during their campaign and subsequent presidential speeches, one being former Democrat President Bill Clinton. Only, Donald J Trump, obtained copyright of the language to promote it as a branding option, a typical businessman's thought pattern.

Another urgent desire has been the freedom of religious belief or Christian ideologies that of which has been under fire, using suppression, or legal exploitation. America's social foundation footing built on faith in God or a higher power. Although there are many different titled religions, with slightly different but similar ideologies, have been under attack by those who wish to either stray away from or no longer find validity in the core teachings of the bible. Many have seen churches or places of worship abandoned, burned, torn down, or converted into something else. Christians have been under attack by atheists who claim a symbolic cross is an invasion of their freedoms, wanting them removed or destroyed, hidden from sight, not giving any thought to those it represented when erected as a monument. Instead of looking the other way, allowing others to have their own beliefs, a small select group manages to cry the loudest, utilizing the legal system, and using liberal progressive thinking, judges win the abilities to infringe upon others. It doesn't seem too fair now.

I have spoken to illegal immigrants, legal working temporary immigrants, H1B Visa holders, those who lost jobs to H1B Visa holders, those on student visas, naturalized citizens, undocumented individuals, people of all races, religious backgrounds, and some with conflicting ideologies while attempting to explain what would be the phenomenal election year 2016. The truth remains the same with ALL, and it boils down to one word, "fairness." One would think this to be a simple and attainable fact in a country of laws, but it is not as simple as it seems. Most feel or view the immigration system as opportunistic, too political, and lacking in legal or financial fairness. As millions emigrated legally to the United States, became naturalized to a country that offered them opportunities unavailable in their natural-born countries. These legal immigrants who migrated to America found the right path they followed diligently with significant financial cost handed out easily to millions who failed to follow the same laws, pay an equal monetary value, or by merit. Most are disgusted with the political gameplay, costing them their jobs and stability.

Although I was too young, my husband, mother, father, uncles, and millions of others were privy to the beginning of the enhanced distrust for government in our country, which exacerbated during the Vietnam era.

The object of military service to your country was to protect your homeland and the freedom of its people, which was not so evident during this time where the draft was instituted, and so many were sent to a foreign country to battle for what, no one still knows. The free love era, the baby boomers, and distrust heightened with protest. Unfortunately, those who were in service and drafted to perform a duty to their country returned to face ridicule, objection, titled baby-killers and did not receive the respect nor recognition for many years to come and even still suffer from the stigma of that time. These service members became part of the distrust group as well. A snowball effect happened, where the United States, by the direct intervention of politically elected leaders, became the protector of the world and intervened whenever possible into other countries' problems for the sake of democracy. America, at this point, was forgetting her people at home who began to bear the brunt of increased tax dollars to fund such interventions and afford the millions of refugees or those seeking asylum.

Slowly but surely, the needs of other country's peoples became first, and of more importance, illegal immigration, and refugee influx without proper vetting was becoming an all-time high along with the enhancement of political correctness. Soon after the PC culture movement, individual civil liberties became select depending upon identity and propagated political correctness in the forefront along with a thwarted view of what was considered the insulting and opinionated perception of what was emotionally hurtful. Therefore, the new requirement being freedom of opinion, views, speech, and beliefs segregationally suppressed.

Remember the old saying, "sticks and stones may break your bones, but names will never hurt you"? Many of us grew up nicknamed, frogs, wops, guineas, pollocks, golden pollocks, micks, slant eyes, krauts, Ricos, wetbacks, Chicano, spics, bible thumpers, chandelier swingers, holy rollers, to name a few. No one took offense, went off the deep end and had to hide in the closet, or come out shooting; many wore it as a badge of honor. Granted, if the terminology or use of slang to differentiate another, the tone of voice would determine if it was in jest or condescension. Now, if you even utter these words today, you will find yourself in the crosshairs of the PC police.

Needless to say, because of the slight percentage and that percentage was small caused the inevitable, "be careful what you say, or else," time in our country. We, as a society, have become so thin-skinned that everything was an offensive comment stated or understated. Civil rights attorneys were having a field day, making plenty off of the PC culture offenders. Businesses were sued because they were uncomfortable with providing services to gay couples for their union or wedding ceremonies, although it conflicted with their religious beliefs; nonetheless, the sharks circled the alleged victims, and the lawsuits came forth with a vengeance.

Throughout the 2016 election, I have had the privilege to interact with and view so many different people ranging from millennials, xennials, retirees, white, black, Asian, Muslim, Hispanic, Jewish all of whom were filled with surprises, controversy and an overabundance of opinion from "Deplorable Deb Reporting from Her Basket" to "Diamond and Silk," a couple of my favorites.

What I experience via social media outlets and by personal interactions was a large amount of disrespect or confusion to understanding the right or freedom of speech taken from the paragraph statement once written by our founders for our constitution was, now being taken out of context and interpreted differently by so many, politicians, media talking heads, and educators alike.

Just when you thought history was just that, history, here comes the most controversial group of its day jumping back in to take a front seat. Early on, in the 2016 campaign process, endorsements are always a talking point for the media play and the candidates to wear as badges. Donald J Trump was endorsed by David Duke, Imperial Wizard of the KKK, on May 2nd, 2016, an endorsement that could not be viewed and as more condemning. No matter how quickly and how many times candidate Trump disavowed this endorsement the mainstream media, Hillary Clinton, her campaign chairs, and sadly then-President Obama would not let it go or pushed the racist, white supremacist narrative to their followers blatantly omitting the simple fact of Trumps' immediate declination or acceptance to the Duke endorsement. The fact of the matter the hypocrisy was full bore on this one as Hillary Clintons' longtime mentors and one of whom she openly and continuously stated she admired; George Soros was a former Klan head. But, of course, we would all come to realize there is a double standard when it comes to Hillary Clinton and her Democrat colleagues. From this point forward, Trump, his supporters, his family, and anyone connected to the Trump name by acquaintance or thought became labeled as racist and a white supremacist, including his black or brown Trump supporters. A simple question to ask would be, how is this logical minded?

As the name-calling continued and identity politics prevailed by propagandist democrats, it became apparent many of those used as political identity tools, could care less what color or nationality another was, they felt we should have moved past this by now. No matter what locale you live in, there will always be someone who still has a bias toward another for one reason or another or just because, generally, without any real logical explanation. It appears as the more controlling and suppressive the liberals became more anger and outrage brewed. Millions of Americans were tired of specified identity categories or to be politically correct, bowing down to the culture changes that now began to invade and control their daily lives.

In general, people want to wake up in the morning, go about their day in peace without conflict or drama. At every turn, there was a new issue that arose, and many felt it was due to the new age of the Democrat political party ideologies. No longer was the democrat party just for the working man as it had been in the past or as it claimed as such. More and more, with each new development, it became apparent that the career politicians were only out for the vote no matter how it came so that they could remain in the seat of control. The poor became poorer, having to set aside what little they had for the sake of illegal aliens and refugees afforded more than they. The middle class slowly became almost non-existent, whereas they too were working harder, giving in more to taxes only to have their money squandered away by the government and its inept frivolous policies.

Many who once worked in factories, were now unemployed, forced to take state and government subsidies, to get by, their pride was taken away. I spoke to people whose homes lost value rapidly and were over-under, they lost their jobs and had to walk away from their financial burdens, feeling it was the only option they had. Many are tired of the lack of American made items, knowing that those products once made in America were better manufactured and lasted longer. Generally, those who were of this thought pattern blamed the unions for becoming too overbearing and costly, causing businesses to close and move out of the country for the cheaper labor force overseas.

Many individuals are angered by the influx of refugees and illegal aliens into the country, where immediate housing was a priority, subsidies automatic, and jobs were given away to these new alien minorities over naturalized or natural-born American citizens. The fiscal benefit or lower employment cost to corporations allows an H1B visa applicant to take precedence in the workforce, with some United States degree holders forced to take jobs outside of their course studies as their desired employment position was no longer available to them. Granted, not one person had an issue with those migrant workers who came here legally each year to work crops, then returned to their native country. No one complained about legal immigrants who were in the country by way of student visas, work visas, green card holders, or those awaiting naturalization.

To US-born, naturalized, and those immigrants are awaiting citizenship, the failure of non-citizens to follow immigration laws is a largely dominant issue. I spoke with a gentleman who had saved for years to come to the United States, leaving Greece. He was going to be sponsored by his uncle, who was already here in the country legally. It took him 17 years overall to afford, make the journey, and become naturalized. Shortly after he became a citizen of the United States, he began driving others to their naturalization ceremonies, primarily in New York state. Another naturalized Hispanic woman, of whom I have mentioned previously in chapter five, came to the US on a work visa, worked her way through the naturalization process, one of her jobs was to act as an interpreter and drive others to polling stations. Both examples of legal or naturalized immigrants mentioned were angry, disappointed, and bothered by the lack of border enforcement and were 100% for the border wall that then-candidate Trump spoke in reference. The southern border was not viewed as racist nor phobic by millions, but as a secure substantive measurement forcing all who wished to enter the United States, come legally, as they both had.

Another sore point was that of battles being fought by our military overseas, the number of veterans living in poverty and lacking medical care. The fact is, these unfortunate circumstances are true and should not be an issue in a country built with so many lives lost trying to ensure the freedoms of others. Most Americans want our men and women home, securing our own country, not those of other countries as a priority. Truth told, our country should have no homeless or poverty as our political leaders claim we are overly wealthy with excess to spare. In general, we should take care of our own before the needs of others around the world, something that has been lacking for quite some time.

Another subject of widespread concern was the high payout of entitlements to welfare or Medicaid recipients across the country, which was inclusive of need-based and fraudulent benefits allocated. The high cost of refugee resettlement programs and asylum seekers that now presented as a large portion of their tax payouts, causing an unwanted increase in tax burdens they forcefully, must attempt to afford.

In a nutshell, those that became known as the "silent majority," "forgotten men and women," the deplorables are those that wish to regain the freedoms, opportunities, and live the almost forgotten American dream they work so hard to achieve and retain. Sad but true, with the past administrations' policies and failures of elected officials to Congress were all but unheard from, until which time that same elected official was up for re-election and would preach change from their podiums of falsehoods.

With the failures of our congressional leaders pushing to uphold our immigration laws already in place, the American people began to feel less safe. Millions began to see double standards as the norm, where they would get a ticket for not wearing a seat belt, yet an illegal alien who faces deportation following a crime or failure to comply with immigration reporting requirements can seek sanctuary in a church. Designated sanctuary states or cities were fast becoming ethically problematic where an illegal alien can cross the southern border, receive housing, food, legal services, and afforded opportunities that they now have a hard time attaining or maintaining for themselves and their families. Immigration reform and abidance of laws is a very long discussion when speaking to most; generally, it is right up at the top 2 spots with radical terrorism, and pro-life issues. Our country is subject to extremist activities, not only those of Islamic terrorists but those radicalized as domestic terrorists having been viewpoint thwarted through indoctrination or propagated hate biased opinion via media and divisive politicians.

WHERE DO WE GO FROM HERE?

Although our country is in a far better place, having been temporarily knocked off the trail of globalism, we are still in a hazardous situation where friends and neighbors are no longer civil, they have taken a detour to hatred based upon misconception and hateful propaganda. If we as a country do not stop and think for even the briefest of moments, we will again encounter a civil war between ourselves. This modern-day civil war will be built upon by falsehoods fed by those who wish to control and divide only for their gratification or political gain. Our educational systems have already taken the history books from the classrooms, therefore, advertently eliminating our past, dictating our future to repeat some of the historical atrocities due to lack of knowledge, comprehension, and understanding by the student.

During my research and many discussions with those of like views and opposing opinions, I found such a hatred for each other or those unknown in disagreement, unlike anything I have ever experienced nor witnessed. The primary blame is not to be placed on our educational system alone, but equally, if not more so on our media outlets and political talking heads. Not a day goes by where even the simplest of speeches are taken out of context by the media outlets but also those entrusted to have the best interests of the American people at hand, the politicians. With educators politicizing their classroom studies in conjunction with the failure to teach historical scenarios in the United States and international history, the student is at a disadvantage to make an educated, broadly viewed decision to the validity of what is presented to them by those seeking to propagate hate or division. A classic comment I grew up with, "knowledge is power, learn everything you can about everything you can, remembering there are two sides to every story, don't believe everything you hear, only half of what you see."

In our current environment, videos clipped to eliminate the full picture, and stories told without a beginning nor an end. Social media has become a tool by those who seek to deceive in this polarized political environment where reactions are quick, anger is immediate, remorse or empathy is absent, respect is negligent, and facts are questionably likely.

While watching speeches, hearings, interviews to their entirety, making sure that every word heard so that I can informatively debate any naysayer who opts to spread negative political propaganda to the public to fit their agenda of the day a blatantly clear factor noted. Although foreign intervention does play a role in our democracy, it is the media and politicians that cause the extremely polarized divide in our country. Never in my lifetime nor any presidency that I have studied has there been such a desire to bring down, chastise, or accuse a sitting president of anything possible, to remove them from office.

There is no rhyme nor reason other than change and change that has been portrayed as dangerous by the media talking heads as well as politicians, such as; (D) Chris Murphy of CT, (D) Richard Blumenthal of CT, (D) Adam Schiff of CA, (D) Nancy Pelosi of CA, (D) Maxine Waters of CA, (D) Elizabeth Warren of MA, (D) Kamala Harris of CA, (D) Chuck Schumer of NY, (D) Corey Booker of NJ, (D) Kirsten Gillibrand of NY, once at the top of the list, now surpassed by another hate-filled, radical group of newly elected politicians. These radicals are extreme left-leaning, divisive, agenda-driven persons, all of whom pose a definitive danger to the peaceful existence of Americans. Those being; Ilhan Omar of MN (D), Rashida Tlaib of MI (D), Alexandria Ocasio-Cortez of NY (D), termed members of the squad. Not only have each of the aforementioned-elected officials blatantly and purposefully chosen to obstruct, resist, and call for divisiveness in our country. They have dared to claim our president treasonous when they act treasonous to the very American people of whom elected them to their positions, every time they fail to work together with the dually elected president and their Republican counterparts. Keeping in mind and not to omit, there are extremist, power-hungry Republicans who are working against the President and the American people as well, one predominantly; Mitt Romney of UT (R).

Although predominantly, I mention Democrat elected officials, it stands to wonder why they are so adamant about castrating a dually elected president who has created jobs, pushed immigration enforcement, and followed through on the promises made on the campaign trail, in addition to those of past presidents. What is it that they are genuinely battling as their obstruction, resistance, and failure to work on a bi-partisan level?

Without meaningful condescension, it would be a question to ask if the systemic institutional factors failing the constituents would come into play as well, whereas it is easy to convince the voters with absurd propaganda as the foundation has already been laid by educational indoctrination? Perhaps.

President Trump calls for a travel ban on Muslim majority countries, resistance Democrats, Chuck Schumer (D), and Elizabeth Warren (D), call for a protest, claim it unconstitutional, and mislead the constituency into believing it is a racist or phobic act. What both willfully fail to mention that president Trumps' predecessor Obama imposed a travel ban on the same countries, and these very countries were those conveyed to the incoming administration during the transition team turnover. Like sheep following the shepherd to slaughter these over the top propagandist, politicians caused a chain reaction of protests with the belief that the incoming president was Islamophobic, and the ban was a "Muslim ban," which is still a partisan battle cry.

Failure to cite that the travel constraints were a ban on the entire country mentioned, which included persons of other faiths or religious beliefs and where known radicalized terrorist cells identified as threatening, is blatantly misleading for political propaganda and division. Granted, the terminology plays a role in the confusion, whereas, Muslim majority triggers the political gameplay by the propagandist to the easily influenced.

The president signs an executive order to remove the healthcare mandate, and the extremist politicians cry out loudly, claiming it is inevitable death to those with pre-existing conditions, promoting fear. When the Republican party held the majority in Congress passed tax cuts across the board, and the minority leader at that time, Nancy Pelosi (D), called it Armageddon and breadcrumbs. To a millionaire politician, an extra $1000 to $2000 extra annual income may appear to be menial, however, to the constituent, it is an additional $80 to $160 per month, more food on the table or heat in the winter.

The first budgetary discussions and vote ended up in a filibuster by the democrat party as they wanted a solution to the ended or expired DACA program. By holding millions of Americans and their families at bay potentially not receiving the necessary funding for special programs all for the sake of illegal alien tagalongs, designated as "dreamers" by the past, Obama administration carried onward by the current liberal democrat party career politicians. Even though the Trump administration offered more amnesty for illegal DACA, pathways to citizenship, it was still not acceptable to the obstructionist Democrats. Ultimately an Omnibus budget was signed, and the filibuster shutdown ended with no real change for either the American people or the designated DACA and their families. As time would continue, the timeline for the DACA program would inevitably expire and no longer be of immediate use for the democrat talking points, thus leaving over 800,000 in the shadows of insecurity.

The Russia narrative of collusion with the Trump campaign was kept alive consistently by the media, Connecticut Senators, Richard Blumenthal (D), and Chris Murphy (D), with their favorite media interview outlets of choice MSNBC and CNN. Although, Senator Blumenthal opts to centralize himself on the Russia story and the no there, there, Senator Murphy bounces from subject to subject of the hour or day to grandstand. Senator Adam Schiff (D), repeatedly announced he had absolute knowledge of collusion between the Trump campaign and Russia, however when pushed for disclosure, he walked back without admission to falsified information. Although the collusion narrative portrayed as valid, truthful, and absolute to the public, no documentation or specific proven details were ever shown. Multiple Democrat senators, including Richard Blumenthal (D), attempted to push for legislation to protect the Muller probe from intervention by the president in an effort for Robert Muller not to be fired.

Half of the country believed that President Trump wishes to fire Robert Muller, and the other half heard the president contradict this claim. With the Democrats seething at the bit, the Muller investigation into Russian collusion finally came to an end with the report of; no Russian collusion found between Russia and Trump.

A pin drop to silence, tears shed by drama journalist, Rachel Maddow. The disbelief was impossible to fathom for those who believed the tall tale they had told; now, a new spin must take place, immediately, that being obstruction of justice. Ironically the once admired Robert Muller was now looked down upon by the Democrat obstructionists as his fair play was not acceptable to the "get rid of Trump" agenda.

An example of political gameplay would be by current Connecticut Senator Chris Murphy (D), who manages to find ways to take credit for the legislative actions or positives of others as his own. Senator Murphy tweets and speaks consistently for the people of Yemen, which appears to be held in higher urgency to him than his constituents in Connecticut or the United States. Senator Murphy posted the following comment on Twitter 7/24/2018, and I quote, "Congress's recent refusal to do our constitutional duty and declare war (Libya, Yemen, ISIS, etc.) risks looking a big green light to a war-hungry executive who might need a manufactured overseas crisis to distract from domestic turmoil. #Iran". The reaction to this was mixed; however, seen as the Senator was upset that the US is not going to war and that Congress should vote for it. The American people are not interested in this by any means. One example of the confusion and fearmongering caused by this politician; the subject list is long and broad for this senator and others like him.

As the call to vote for the Democrats to regain control, our former first lady, Michelle Obama, was hot on the 2018 mid-term campaign trail with her "your vote is your voice," #WhenWeAllVote, we all do better narrative. The same former first lady who stated, "women who didn't vote for Hillary Clinton and voted for Donald J Trump, had no voice, failed to do their civic duty, and were controlled by the men in their lives." The same former first lady who many of us wonder if she voted for Hillary Clinton against her husband Barrack in the primaries for the 2008 presidential run, or was her voice silent then?

Although I have targeted Democrats primarily, many of the Republicans are not far behind in criticism, titled the "never-trumpers" located within the GOP. Failures by both parties to hear or acknowledge the constituencies outcries can be exemplified when referring to Hillary Clinton, whereas the same holds for many of the currently elected political heads, of whom are detached from the people. The views and beliefs of millions across the country collectively agree that politicians have failed to protect them, prefer identity politics over action politics, fail to hear the distressed cries from the hardworking, overtaxed, oppressed people of the United States. When candidate Hillary Clinton calling millions of Americans deplorable because they differed in viewpoints of the direction of the country disagreeing with her alleged policies, the currently elected Democrat politicians are doing the same were the pleas of America's children are falling on deaf ears.

The where and how candidate Donald J Trump became the dually elected president of the United States, as he heard the people, he kept his finger on the pulse of America and realized this is a battle he wanted to fight and would inevitably win. This pied piper of reason, cut across the political grain of the status quo, shaking up every aspect of the political scene possible. One could look at this businessman's insight as a salesman's ability to sell a product he knew very well, himself. The sale of this intimate product was a great hit with the people and remains still, even though the endless criticisms.

Still today, it can be heard that Russia influenced the 2016 presidential election with propaganda; however, the fact is the American people found someone to listen to them and listen he did. Hillary Clinton still blames anyone and everyone, the obstructionist democrats still blame Russia and the fictitious collusion story, never looking within nor into the looking glass, seeing that they are the reason for failure to win the election. Not only was it the failures of the Democrat candidate, but the lack of care and consideration for the heartbeat of America, the people. We the people made this happen, not Russia, not any other foreign entity, no propaganda, the people, the same people whose ancestors blood flows strongly through their veins, the voices of the past telling them to stand up and fight for their country just as they did throughout the decades.

It will continue to be a fight for our freedoms, and this fight will never end. However, we as a country cannot afford to back down from this battle, and we must prevail. Our constitution, written by our founding fathers, having the foresight that this day may come, must be adhered to. It would be in the best interest of the obstructionist political heads to sit up and pay attention or be cast aside, left to wonder in a cloudy existence, asking themselves, why and how.

ILLOGICALLY LOGICAL

I'm sure that I am not the only one to see the illogical or hypocritical thought processes around us every day. My husband and I went to an eatery that we go to while we are at the boat during the summer. We ordered from the young waitress, who brought us our drinks; however, when asked for a straw, she began to lecture us on the "straws suck" rule. After laughing, we left it at that. Another futile attempt at those who are a party to the destruction taking a hypocritical stand to change it. Hence, a table sign that I copied verbatim and read as follows:

Straws Suck…
We are joining a global movement to
"refuse the straw."
from our landfills, streams & oceans.

At least 2.5 trillion plastic particles are
currently floating in the ocean

Many animals, including turtles, whales and
fish we eat, dies from eating plastic

The plastic debris known as the
"Great Pacific Garbage Patch"
Has increased by 100 times in the
last 40 years!

We could wrap the earth 2.5 times per day
with our plastic straw usage.

Our intention is not to inconvenience our
guest, but such a simple act can have a
positive effect on our planet!
Every little bit helps!
Thank you for your willingness.

As we are on the Atlantic coast, one fact our waitress didn't know. What happens to the disabled, elderly, or messy children who cannot manage without the use of a straw? Are they to be alienated from partaking in beverages at these "no straw" establishments? On the contrary, we now have the creation of the "metal straw," streamlined, straight, or bent. So instead of a plastic straw that should be incinerated, we are to carry our private metal object to suck through. This finely designed replacement comes with its warning label as you may not run with it, be careful when using it as you may break your tooth or fracture your dentures, if not properly sterilized may harbor harmful bacteria, with a longer decomposition lifetime. Savvy, isn't it? And by the way, you may not take it on a plane with you as it is considered a dangerous object, like a knife which may impale another. Before you know it, the eco-friendly pasta straw, which has taken Europe by straw, will be the next craze to hit our eateries. The only potential downfall or question would be, does it come, gluten-free?

Factually, it is a society that causes this litter issue and not just in the USA, and it is an effect felt global. However, activists and politicians make it the fault and financial burden of the United States taxpayers to correct the ineptitudes or callousness of others here and abroad. We find ourselves in the debate of whether it is the fault of the inanimate object or the human element which discards the object inappropriately. Ironically, the annual spring break events create temporary clean up jobs or overtime hours for crews tasked with the litter pick up or control for callous students who litter excessively. In 2018 the government faced a lengthy shut down due to budgetary refusals to compromise, causing state parks across the country to go unmanned for a short period. With no visual or physical human in attendance, some in the general populous found it acceptable to utilize these parks as their waste dumping ground. With the help of volunteers who respected and cared for the preservation of these parks, the discarded rubbish was picked up and removed. If those conscientious individuals had not taken it upon themselves to pick up after the careless, there would be a trash heap, of course, with flies and maggots, another hypocritical subject for climate activists to complain about. These, at times over the top hypocritical climate activists, have descended upon cities and towns, including Washington, DC, to promote their views of climate change, only to leave behind a field of litter in their wake. The debate for and against a simple plastic straw, or any other target unit, is one that may not save the world nor make that great an impact if the human element is not held accountable for its callous actions.

As the narrative states, "plastic particles," you can barely look around you without almost 80% or more of your everyday products made from plastic or some composite of plastic. The hypocrisy of those that lobby for the ban on plastic straws can be seen in the failures to cease the use of 6-pack holders that once held their cans left on the spring break beach, or the side of the road, and the ATM cards with which the beverages purchased. Keep in mind the cellphones that were used to text or call everyone where to hook up must cease to exist or be banned as well.

If we are to control or change the overbearing amount of garbage that is dumped in the oceans daily, we must first work on educating other nations on the use of incinerators, but then again, those same activists or others will start complaining about acid rain or the fumes put into the atmosphere to burn. Common sense would tell you, don't litter, pick up your crap, put it in the garbage can, or take it with you.

What if we ban "all" forms of plastic, including credit cards and ATM cards, not only will we hinder identity theft, we will go back to a cash society, many of these common core math students will need to learn simple math and be able to count change for themselves without that plastic-encased computer screen with a calculator app. Millennials or Xennials may learn how to budget and the meaning of a dollar. Of course, it will never happen, disposable is in and here to stay; after all, it is not the same as a straw, right?

Just like electric cars, fuel-efficient, however, the thought of what happens to the expired or rotten batteries to run these electronic marvels is not of concern even though the damage to the environment is a priority. The thought is a decrease in the carbon footprint of a vehicle, when mechanically speaking, 1993 gas burning Volvo 940 wagon will have a similar if not less of an overall impact than that of the electric-powered Toyota Prius with its toxically corrosive battery components in the landfill.

Hypocritically former President Obama entered the United States into the Paris Climate Accord Agreement yet fashioned a multicar motorcade in similarity to all other presidents. Even the critical, know all elites in Hollywood, protest, lobby, and advocate for Climate Change while they look down on the tiny houses and fields from their private jets, tweeting from their cellphones, and sell their records, cd's, and tapes in plastic cases. Whatever it takes, right?

How about the never-ending gun debate, it is the guns fault, ban all guns, so they won't get up one morning and kill someone. So many politicians, primarily Democrat, believe that more gun laws will prevent mass shootings. These illogically logical extremists have even convinced their base followers that this is true. They never explain that more times than none, the gun used in a mass shooting belongs to another individual was obtained illegally or retrofitted illegally. Hardly heard is rhetoric preached by any politician or activist address the root issue, and that it is the individual who chose to make that decision and utilize that firearm. Rarely do you hear about the breakdown in law enforcement communications or psychosocial changes that prompt the breaking point in an individual to cross the line of right versus wrong. Granted our founding fathers did not expect that a rapid-fire gun would be created, however, they did have to foresight to know that the people of this nation would one day be faced with a government that no longer works for them, so they made the 2nd amendment as a top priority. The thought pattern of our founding fathers was to keep the people with rights to bear arms, which are compatible with those of the government, therefore maintaining a fair battleground.

At the shoreline, boating logic never fails to surprise as well. You must go through a classroom and written exam boater safety course to maneuver anything that has a motor on it. However, you do not have to take a driving test. Just like the driver of that massive motorhome that takes out every mailbox, the boater of a large craft can take out every dingy or run into every other boat because they answered correctly on the exam yet never presented practical knowledge abilities on the water.

We need to wear our seatbelts or face a fine. However, we can't choose our healthcare plans. Some of us spend thousands of dollars for an education, receive our degrees proudly when another gets an honorary degree without stepping into a classroom or dropping a dime just because of who they know, who their parent may be or whatever their life identity choice is at the time.

Sad but true, the simplicity of life is no more, and we live in such a complicated country surrounded by an incredibly diverse global existence.

One will find themselves scratching their head from time to time in bewilderment and question themselves what is normal or not, right or wrong, with absolute utter headache creating confusion.

From fart bags on cows to chicken diapers, what in the world have we become? We send rockets into space to conveniently place satellites so we can chat on our smartphones, watch tv anywhere we see fit, but we must all become vegans never to eat a hearty steak because cows cause too much damage to the ozone with their emission of methane gas. Really?

On a day to day basis logic eludes the simplest of tasks, causing many of us to wonder if we are in an altered reality or if somehow the scene where Marty and Doc Brown must go back to the future to get the time continuum to align again is, in fact, a documented video in history.

Even now, as we exchange ideas and opinions, our elected officials are again attempting to undo the results of the 2016 dually elected president, of whom they claim illegitimate, therefore, calling the will of the people illegitimate. The porn star narrative failed along with the Russia collusion allegations. Now we have a propagated "quid pro quo" with Ukraine; therefore, an impeachment inquiry must be made. Sadly, many Americans do not have the time to hang on every detail, thus can easily be misled. The Democrat party is holding interviews behind closed doors, refusing access to their Republican counterparts, only giving the American people the calculated narrative information they wish them to receive. These actions are against the constitutional right of due process, yet the Democrat party of today will cite that we are in a constitutional crisis by President Trump and the Republican party, while they are in violation.

Our founding fathers failed to see that money and power create a dangerous group of future politicians who are held accountable only by themselves if they see fit. These very out of control, pedestal topping individuals can only be voted out of office by their constituencies if their voters are made aware of their ineptitudes, and improprieties. A sad state of affairs we are in.

As history would show, the New Era Democrat Party, which held the majority control in the House of Representatives, would ultimately succeed in their quest to vote for articles to formally impeach President Trump. This impeachment vote would be by partisan means only and not by unanimous vote. Tulsi Gabbard (D) of Hawaii, would vote "present" as she did not consciously believe those actions by the sitting president were critical enough to warrant impeachment. Two Democrats voted with Republicans not to impeach, one of them Collin Peterson (D) of Minnesota, and Jeff Van Drew (D) of New Jersey. One other Jared Golden (D) of Maine voted to impeach under the article of abuse of power, but not for obstructing Congress.

After all that had been said and portrayed, the American people would come to see the malicious nature of the Democrat party of today. Those few in opposition represent the Democrat party of yesterday, or the JFK Democrats, more logical, fair, and balanced. By the impeachment battle cries and promises made by Representatives Rashida Tlaib and Maxine Waters to the screen test moment of; Adam Schiff who narrated his rendition of the Ukraine call, later walking it back as joking, the American people witnessed an actual crisis to our democracy and violation of our constitutional due process.

After the votes in the Democrat majority held House of Representatives were cast, Speaker Nancy Pelosi announced the results, graciously slamming the gavel. History written with a permanent tarnish had been placed upon the peoples' president. Not one Republican voted, all argued before Congress the failures of the process and lack of constitutionality, proving moot to change. The next step would be for Speaker Pelosi to forward these articles of accusation and condemnation to the Senate. Conveniently, the holiday recess had begun, and no work would be conducted until January 2020. As with the trade deal with Canada and Mexico, known as the USMCA, those articles would sit on Speaker Pelosi's desk until she deemed fit to forward them constitutionally to the Senate.

The hypocrisies are abundant as the Democrat Party minus a select few voted to impeach a president who was consistently improving the economic stability of the country, creating jobs, negotiating favorable trade deals, reinforcing the strength of our military, and importantly negotiating the release and return home of our citizens held captive in other countries since the Obama administration.

The sad reality is the Trump administration's positives, which are seldom reported by the mainstream media outlets and overshadowed by the political gameplay. Millions of Americans have been propagated to hate what they do not know is favorable to the country due to falsehoods and misrepresentations of opinion. Without accurate facts or fairness to reporting, the American people are at a disservice to make an educated opinion themselves, whether positive or negative.

CHILD REARING 101-A
PASS OR FAIL?

Shortly after the initiation of the hyper-exaggerated PC movement, the modern advancements on how to raise or discipline your child timeline began, which itself caused many of the problems we have today. Again, due to a small percentage of overbearing, overly aggressive parental disciplinarians, children were being taught in schools that, "if your parent spanks you, you feel threatened, or you feel in danger, call the police," hence the new child-rearing methodology was force-fed to the American parent by those deemed experts.

As children, we learn with boundaries, guidelines, and gain respect for others, ourselves, and elders. The limitations or guidelines taught to the young generally carry into adult lives. Now the child can manipulate a situation justifying the instance of controlling the parent with a potential threat of arrest or incarceration, basically because they don't like the discipline outcome or requirement by the parent or older guardian. Parents found themselves in a more strained atmosphere and lax on their discipline to prevent conflict or potential negative repercussions. This methodology didn't turn out so well as we see the effects of the societal and parental disciplinary failures today with the unruly, out-of-control young adults we deal with now.

Remember standing in the corner when you acted out in class? I had this opportunity a time or two where the location to stand silently in the corner was by the pencil sharpener, so my friends in class usually came up more often to sharpen their pencils and say "hi." To stand in the corner today and time-outs now are forms of harmful isolation and are believed to expose children to ridicule, so we don't do it anymore. How about stay at the table until you finish your dinner? It is abusive because you are force-feeding your child. I remember staying at the table being forced to eat baked beans, which I absolutely hated. I sat at the table for some time until I figured out that if I stuck them under the chair cushion when no one was looking, this made the appearance or so it seemed as if I gave in, and I ate them. Ultimately when the chair cushion was changed, it was then discovered where my beans went, so my grandmother conceded. A spanking is unheard of, even a tap on the bum is considered an invasion of space or physical abuse.

A new, more ludicrous example of childcare or rearing is that of; Deanne Carson, a sexuality educator in Australia who believes that you should ask the baby if they want their nappy or diaper changed and if they don't, you shouldn't because it was a violation or offensive. Really? If you walk into the emergency room or your doctors' office with that same baby here in the United States and it has a severe diaper rash, what are you going to say, "the baby told me not too." You would be accused and subsequently charged with child neglect in a heartbeat. Many of us, old school parents, change the diapers often or let them run around butt naked. Sometimes they run around butt naked whether we like it or not, as my son did many a time until I started putting his clothes on backward.

A hug rewards terrible behavior, and ultimately negative behavior outbursts viewed the ultimate failure on the part of the adult, therefore giving in and allowing the child to do whatever it so wishes, inevitably a counter-productive methodology of teaching boundaries and respect. Some child psychologists would state this was a positive reinforcement method; in opposition, many would argue the point considering the actions of those disciplinary measures a failure, exemplified by many of the youth today.

Although we can claim sole burden upon the parent or guardian for the unruly child, yet we must take into consideration the economic strains that society places causing the primary influences to be outside sources in a daycare setting or other to family influence. The days of the stay at home guardian are minimal as the cost of maintaining the home has become financially burdensome.

Once the child entered the educational system, they are influenced by positive and negative variables dependent upon the national locales' ideologies. An era of presumed or "expert" determined attention-deficit categories were made placing many children in the class of a Ritalin dependent control group, claiming they were attention deficient. This once infamous way of controlling the unruly child decades later deemed detrimental.

My little cousin, not so small today, was a toddler when she was finally taken from her mother and placed in the care of my uncle and his then-wife. Unfortunately, for her, this was not the best scenario, and now, years later, the effects are apparent. With the life situations this child was placed in, it was, in my belief, the dominant reasoning behind her lack of discipline, yet she became the product of the Ritalin group by those who were in the dark of her life circumstances.

At times, overdramatic guardians and attorneys succeeded in propagating fear and control onto the educational system from educators to administrators, employing, lawsuits claiming discriminatory actions or presumed violations on the child when disciplined for unacceptable behavior. The intolerable became the controlling norm in the classroom, and the educators' ability to maintain a positive learning environment became a balance upon the tightrope, where one disruption caused all to fall, and they were provided no safety net. No more was respectful demands, disciplinary concerns for the student, only the knowledge of superiority and dictation of the classroom events. The healthy balance was diminishing. Without boundaries and discipline, education became moot and a place for your child of any age to have daily access to a new form of taxpayer-funded daycare.

The balance needed to become more productive, cost-effective, presumed need-based; hence, the educator becomes the indoctrinator by utilizing the impression that the child was a free-thinker and must express themselves. Instead of boundaries, respect, and discipline, strive to learn methodology replaced with a positively reinforced everyone gets a participation trophy ideology. No more achieve to be the best, accel on strengths, try to grasp the brass ring. Without the strong influences of those determined parents and guardians, we would have a much larger generation of indoctrinated bare minimum thinkers, clueless to their surroundings, led by falsehoods, and propagated with pseudo-life survival skills both mentally and physically.

On the educational platform, sociology took priority over the US and American history; therefore, becoming minimalized as necessary, due to the common core curriculum and adherence to the changing globalist era. I, as well as many other parents, chose to educate our children at home, teaching them the history of the country they live in and its inception. If one does not know your country's history, you are doomed to repeat the atrocities of the past.

History has now shown to repeat itself, look at our country today within the titled field of racism. The divisions and racial tensions are not those that never disappeared but those of propagated opinion hate by political talking heads and media outlets. We have black commentators pushing white supremacy, or white-lash, calling on the predictable race card at every turn even when hypocritically it is an opposing view of another with the same skin pigmentation. Of course, when this occurs and is called out, they claim blinding by right-wing conservatives, or they have abandoned their race. We have liberals with or without higher education condemning conservatives with or without equal or higher education as the "less than smart" Trump base, only because there are opposing views.

The terminology of racism is flippantly used when millions speak in unison with the president about border control and the desire for people to come to the U.S. legally or become documented and naturalized to the country that millions of others have, including the families of migrants, refugees, and immigrants before them. Immigration has become thwarted in view where legality and laws are unbalanced used only as a vote gaining talking point for Democrats to the generationally indoctrinated global socialist group.

With the teaching of our country's history, you learn respect for the flag, our veterans, and understand those who made the difficult passage to come to America fleeing from tyranny. We cannot express the importance of the significance and symbolism of "lady liberty." Our most prominent recognizable symbol of freedom utilized as a prop on July 4th, 2018, in an anti-ICE protest by; Patricia Okoumou, an immigrant from the Democratic Republic of Congo. Later it would be known that this woman had an innate hatred toward the country she now called her home and acted out based upon a statement made by a radical activist and small-time producer; Michael Moore. In years past, this action would have been considered treasonous, and her citizenship would have been taken away, therefore placing her up for deportation back to her home country. Now, numerous individuals surround her in an effort of protection, calling her actions freedom of speech or expression, never acknowledging that she placed many in danger while attempting to rescue her or get her down off the statue base and she disrupted the day for many of whom came to see this icon of freedom.

So many protesters today do not even know the actual reason for the American Civil War battle, where it was fought, who won, and why. Those who haven't been taught history feel it was only about slavery. I have had some individuals tell me that it was the fault of the Republicans, little did they know Abraham Lincoln was a Republican and the president responsible for the Emancipation Proclamation. These individuals who lacked historical teaching on this subject did not know that the US was segregated, and the most prominent advocate for slavery back then was a Democrat. Even with the facts presented, they will inevitably tell you that you are lying.

Many protesters today believe the Confederate flag is that of racism, hate, and bigotry, whereas it is part of not only America's growth history but that of another's family history, who values the stars and bars in a different view. The fact is, those that know the history of our country, its trials and tribulations have more of an understanding and acknowledge the historical significance.

When my mother-in-law passed away, the family opted to drape her casket with the Confederate flag as it was her wish, and an integral part of her family history being from the State of Virginia. The service went on as usual, and the minister from the Baptist church she had attended was an incredible minister, a black woman who spoke eloquently and kindly about her, never once showing any concern over this symbol of history, nor presuming or casting judgment. It boils down to how you educate at home, whether it be progressive history with an understanding of the past or divisive indoctrination of hate never forgotten.

Thousands viewed witnessed effects of questionable child-rearing, discipline, and teaching respect for others via a Facebook video posted by what was now the era of 15 minutes of fame or the "look at me" acting out crowd. On January 5, 2017, a pathetically sad situation where four young black individuals bound and beat a white special needs man. These kids or age defined young adults, bound and beat this defenseless individual forcing him to recite and admit that it was all "Trumps' fault, fuck Trump, hate Trump." How sad our society has become, where an individual is unable to have their views and beliefs or support someone they choose, for whatever reason. Social media was ablaze with racial accusations whereas the skin color nor race was the issue here, this group of disrespectful kids couldn't manage to gang up on anyone or group other than one who is weaker than they are in a pathetic display of hate. And they speak of bullying?

Our country has again become more focused on division and racism than unity. The term or label "racist" is thrown around so lightly and no longer based upon actual skin color as it was back throughout the struggles of the pre and post-civil war era. Education at home on the historical significance of changes pre-liberal hysteria is necessary for our children to understand all sides and not fall to the one path indoctrination by our liberal common core schools, therefore making them able to make better decisions based on aggregate data not just through hypocrisy from others. In some cases, the home life of either side of racial extremism can be further fortified by outside educational influences received in the school setting or dominant societal impacts. Our children are educational sponges soaking up whatever knowledge is poured out to them; the more authoritative the view flow, the favorable or adverse the life choice effect becomes.

A Facebook post by David Yankovich @DavidYankovich states, "We hate Donald Trump-like you hated President Obama. However, we hate Trump because he is racist; you hated Obama because you are racist". Nowhere in this tweet does it state the fact of good versus poor policy issues and societal changes that many Americas still have and still face; therefore, disagreement is now constituted as "racism."

Racism has taken on a meaning unlike anything we have ever known it to be, and it has been propagated by outside sources to mean so much more than it should. As a parent, we must teach our children strength, compassion, respect, and to have an open mind listening to all sides of a story before making a judgment or action. So many self-proclaimed or presumed experts feel they can tell you the best way to raise your child, many forcefully attempt to do so; however, it does not always mean they are right.

Growing up, we went to church, learned of God, good and evil. We learned of the penalties for wrongdoing and the fear of condemnation, guilt, penance, and redemption. Family dinners were a time to gather, catch up on the days' events and strengthen the bond between all; now we have busy work schedules, take out, fast food, text messaging, the family units are falling further apart barely tethered, sometimes together for that Easter Sunday service or Christmas vigil.

Granted, not all of us are perfect parents; we all make mistakes. However, if we manage to keep our children busy enough to stay out of trouble and off drugs, we are doing well. If we teach them to survive on their own, prosper without us as a constant financial institution or crutch, we succeeded. A good parent lets their children get dirty, use their imagination, and shows their children all the beautiful, amazing things this world has to offer, not necessarily through constant travel as many can't afford lavish trips, but right in your back yard.

Remember the days of staying outside until the lightning bugs came out, catching them in a jar? How about sleeping in a tent in the back yard, playing games, riding your bike, making snow angels, snowball fights, falling, skinning your knee to get back up and do it again even though it hurt like hell? Now kids play video games, watch tv, spend endless hours on social media, what are they experiencing or learning as the essential tools for future survival?

We, as a society, need to get back to the teaching of humility and respect, not just for others but ourselves. Donald Trump Jr's., parenting skills are still being criticized with an angry backlash from a tweeted picture of his daughter with a half-full pumpkin Halloween candy bucket. This simple example of half full versus half empty philosophy was a rebuttal filled with those thinking this was an example of a spoiled child with greed instead of the balance of the narrative explaining that much of the candy was given away. This narrative was viewed as a jealous tantrum by those who feel someone from a billionaire family cannot teach their children humility when the opposite is exact, hence those whose bucket is half empty. The narrative's oppositional view was when you have extra, give it to someone who has less; thus, the bucket is half full, therefore share.

I, too, faced criticism by others when my son was younger. He was a Christmas week baby, and unfortunately for those born on or close to December 25th, sometimes are cheated with a birthday slash Christmas present. When he was a little tyke, I would do as most parents do invite just about everyone to a birthday gala, inevitably going overboard. This one birthday, my son had received numerous presents from the family, with one duplication. As everyone stood around watching him open his presents, waiting for his excitement and look of surprise, he came to one that his aunt had given him. Unfortunately, he had already opened a similar package that contained the same play toy. He, up to that point, laughed, smiled, said thank you every time, except this time. Sadly, his comment was a deep sigh of disgust, which was followed with, "I already got this; take it back." No, thank you. I saw the sadness this caused to his aunt, as this was her gift, one that she thought would be great for him. I, on the other side, was highly disappointed in his actions. After everyone had departed, I asked him to help me tidy up and put his new toys into one pile, which he did diligently. We sat down together to view all that he had received, and I asked him to think carefully and find what was his most favorite of all that he had received that day, which he did. I then told him to go take it from the pile he had created, then asked, "are you sure this is your most favorite?" which he agreed. He then asked me, "Mama, can I play with the rest now?". I responded, "No, you may not." Confused, he asked, "why?". And then I explained to him what his comment and actions had done earlier in the day, along with why the rest of his toys would be given to children less fortunate than him for Christmas. Although I was highly criticized for my actions, this one year taught my son a lesson that he still carries with him today. Not only did he appear spoiled, but he also showed signs of being ungrateful that day. My lesson was of compassion and empathy for others who give of themselves and those less fortunate. I could have just allowed this event to pass, forgotten without reminder, but then again, what would the lesson have been? As we were boxing the rest of the toys, he began to add in a few more from his toy box so that we could have more to bring to the toy drive in town. My little man, although age 4, stated to me, "mama, I thought about it, I don't need all these toys. Can I call auntie and say thank you?". With pride, I responded with his nickname, "of course, baby puppy."

The point is, I am far from a millionaire, let alone billionaire, my lesson to my son was no different than that of Donald Trump Jr's to his daughter. The teachings of humility and compassion begin at a young age, and the examples we show or explain to our children will be carried with them later in life. Although, as we grow into adults, there is a fine line to tow between respect for another, compassion, and empathy for those less fortunate, along with humility, never believing you are better than anyone. One common rule that my memere always preached to us all was that, when you feel you have it so terrible, always remember, there is someone, which is far worse off than you are, care for your family, show compassion for others and help if you have the extra means to do so.

HE SAID WHAT?

As with any political battle, mud-slinging is always at its all-time high. We as American voters were inundated with the narratives spewed of the Trump, Billy Bush audio or hot mike tape that came out, where then-candidate Trump said some lewd comments regarding some of the females he had encountered or interacted with in the past, obviously being "egged on," by Billy Bush. To some, this was the ultimate insult, and from that point forward, he was misogynistic, and so were his supporters, male and female alike. To some, these comments were a moot and benign point. To others, like myself, this was "locker room" chatter and not a deal-breaker as far as candidacy validation. Many a time, I was asked why I was not offended, what my opinion was, and if my mind changed at any time. This audiotape was blatantly apparent that it was typical guy talk, much like that of what some women say about that hellaciously cute guy in tight jeans as he walks past them. If it were not a hot mike situation, no one would have been the wiser.

The presidential opponent, Hillary Clinton, chose to monopolize on the hot mike event to deter from her email scandal and past improprieties that continued to surface. Hillary Clinton never wavered or let up, even though she planned on bringing her husband, former President Bill Clinton back into the White House. The same President Bill Clinton of whom faced impeachment for lying to Congress regarding his sex scandal while in office. Although Bill Clinton was later acquitted of wrongdoing and the impeachment did not stick, the Clintons suffered financial burdens due to accusations, litigations and ordered victim settlement.

With all this said, the typical Trump supporter and many of whom are women, did not wholeheartedly support him as the politically correct candidate. However, they all want the same thing, enforcement of immigration laws, the deportation of criminals, tax reform, taxes paid to go to infrastructure, business regulation reform, border security and protections, revision of taxpayer-funded subsidies encompassed through welfare reform. Not forgetting the end to the Obamacare or ACA mandate, freedom of choice for medical care again, assurance of vetting procedures for refugees brought to this country, the end of double standards for wealthy politicians and other elitists who have put themselves above the law. Other top-priority issues involve veterans' care and oversight as a significant issue, reform of the education system with the elimination of the common core, and abilities for Americans to achieve the "American Dream" once again, no longer affording it for others before themselves.

So many that I spoke with despise or did not wish to press #1 for English. Our country should not have to change our language abilities to accommodate those who refuse to assimilate or neglect to learn our primary language when they wish to stay here in this country. I have observed many different scenarios of the alleged language barrier issue and have been told stories regarding the choice of language use in our country.

In civil or criminal court proceedings, there is a Spanish interpreter present of whom will act as a liaison for someone who alleges they do not speak nor understand English, every case that I witnessed, the same individual who needed that interpreter, left the courtroom and was out in the hallway during a recess speaking proficient English. The clear view of selective communication and understanding was dependent upon the charges imposed upon that individual and their attempt to gain leniency from the court through a portrayed presumptive debilitation.

Another example was when a group of individuals returned to the fishing dock in Mystic some years ago, where they were greeted by the local game warden of whom asked if anyone spoke English to address the illegal short fish that they caught. All present shook their heads in denial of understanding or ability, when the game warden changed the narrative to a seizure of their boat, fishing gear, towing their vehicle, and arresting all involved bringing them to jail until an interpreter could be located, amazingly they had a complete understanding and English was miraculously easy for them.

When my grandparents came to this country, they learned the language, as did my husbands' family; there was no requirement to learn a second language to make others feel welcome. If you planned to move to

Mexico and live out your life, you would learn the language; you wouldn't force them to learn English or your native tongue.

Then-candidate now president Trump agrees with millions of Americans tired of pressing #1 for English, choosing what language you want your ATM transaction to be displayed. What about those who are blind and only read braille in English are they to be left out and not get any cash from that same ATM?

Many a time president Trump will still acknowledge that some of those crossing our southern border are not the best of the best, are bad hombres, rapists and killers, all comments taken out of context and transformed into meanings of bigotry, hatred, and racism. Factual data shows gang members, MS-13, those with sociopathic tendencies, criminals, rapists, drug and child traffickers, radical extremists, and convicted murderers have infiltrated caravans and migrant groups, in an effort, to gain admittance to the United States. Trump also specifies that not all people crossing the borders or migrating here are bad people. However, all who want to come to the United States are welcome but must do so legally. To require alien individuals to follow a country's legal requirements is far from the propagated negative view of anything other than law enforcement and protection of the country's legal citizens.

No matter what Trump says, he is wrong. He says that we are getting screwed by China on trade, backs out of deals, imposes tariffs, renegotiates deals that were not favorable to the U.S., he is picking fights, insulting, causing hate, even though many of these changes are proving to be beneficial.

One of the consistent "never Trumper" video snip-it or comments that float around occasionally is that of then-candidate Trump mocking Ted Cruz. The narrative changed to him mocking a reporter who was disabled, all who witnessed this play-acting and comment by candidate Trump were privy to the actual reference and meaning of what he intended to portray. However, even though debunked with clarification, the media play and political slander to suit the propagated hate agenda prevails on the weak-minded, even with the full context video presented to them.

Donald J Trump is not an eloquent speaker like Barack Hussein Obama, not all people, politicians, nor media journalists are eloquent speakers themselves, yet command perfection from Trump when they are deficient. My memere always told me to "shoot from the hip," "say what you mean, and people will either respect you for it or hate you for it; either way, they will know where you stand." I have tried to live by this and tend to speak my mind often, good, bad, or indifferent, many a time without filter now that I am much older. Must be an age thing. Our current President is our president because he is who he is, speaks as he speaks, no filter, no games, no condescension. Donald J Trump, related to the millions of Americans on their platform, with respect for their American values, desires for freedom, and with many, off-the-cuff, crazy comments and a few, "what the hell," they all knew this man was cut from a different political cloth, believed in the decades-old core values of America, and believed in them, hearing their concerns. Besides, one of his phrases to the black community was, "what the hell do you have to lose?", well, the votes came in across all races, ethnicities, and beliefs and so far, so good, to date we are all winning, prospering again, with exception to healthcare and immigration reforms.

The obstructionist, resistance politicians, refuse to work with this dually elected president, Trump, on any level with the clear view to millions of their constituents that they are willing to sacrifice the country and its people at all costs to deny this administration any positive movement or betterment. It should be a question to all as to why, when all others before had little to no roadblocks, stonewalling, or opposition for the very same America first agendas pushed forward by previous presidential administrations. The very #resistance, obstructionist, propaganda politicians who push back are the same politicians who lobbied for the same plans for the people before. So why now? What is the ultimate intention or goal for them?

Even with the propagated negativity, I see more happy faces, hear more positive stories from everyday working-class people who are finally working again, getting more back in their paychecks, and have renewed hope. People other than the obstructionist, resistance political talking heads, and extremist protesters are happier, more positive. People are spending more money, taking more risks, and say they are feeling better about the country every day, however still concerned about the propagated division.

As long as we all stay strong, hold fast to our American roots, abide by our constitution, we will survive. If we the people do not stand firm against those obstructionist & resistance fighters, we will ultimately lose our country to extreme left radicalization. There is a new danger to the United States and the American people, not that of nuclear bombs, mass shootings, or global warming; it is socialism coupled with American elitist globalism.

THE "NOT SO" SILENT MAJORITY

For the most part, those who became the no longer, "the silent majority" were those who wanted their backs to hurt no more from working so hard and giving up always for those throughout the world, to those illegally residing within their own country and those who have grown accustomed to the government-subsidized system of financial enabling paid for by their hard-earned tax dollars. These supporters want to fly their American flag on their houses and within their yards without someone telling them to take it down. They are tired of seeing someone stomp or burn their flag in protest without suffering ramifications that are covered by our current laws, not hide behind the protest as freedom of speech when it is a blatant disrespect to those who fought and still fight for these freedoms.

The safeties and securities of the country and its people were viewed at risk, more so in 2016 than ever before. The American people were crying out against what they perceived as the lack of concern for them and the country during the prior eight years under the Obama administration. What has now become the "new era" democrat party is that which embodies more interest over globalism than that of the country they were elected to serve. Each time an illegal crossed the southern border, or a refugee entered the country without being properly vetted, there is a question of safety being violated. Most refugees have conveyed that they prefer to stay in their home countries on native land, surrounded by what is familiar, along with military support for their protection assistance in designated safe zones. Not all wish to come to America; unlike the belief of some, many do not like change, and at most times, the unknown is far worse to them than the terrorist looking to kill or enslave them.

Many immigrants who went through the process to become naturalized citizens of the United States are fed up, frustrated, and sickened by the lack of oversight for illegal aliens in the country. Illegal immigration along with the failure to enforce the laws requiring illegal individuals to maintain their whereabouts or circumvention of deportation requirements, border jumping, sanctuary cities, and Trust Act states, visa expirations, oversight of refugees to become citizens, renewals of H1B visas, loss of jobs due to cheaper labor by hiring an H1B visa holder, are all areas of continual concern. Programs such as DACA, mass amnesty, bulk gratis naturalization, sanctuary churches, or blind eye government overstepping the laws, are viewed as a push back and insulting those who emigrated here legally, remained legal, and proudly became naturalized as U.S. citizens.

One sure way to tug at the heartstrings of the American people is to show them a crying or distressed child. Some years ago, I dated an Army Ranger who told me as soon as the news stations begin to show women and children, he would be deployed and, at times, without warning, how true this was. The concerning aspect to those at home waiting to see if the one they cared for was safe or would return, as many of those children they were leaving to fight for were taught to hate Americans and the ideologies of the United States. From the time children are cognitive, they are convinced to think of American soldiers as enemies, forced to act as human bombs walking up to our soldiers casually without concern until many of our servicemen and women are blown up or killed. This wartime mindset has changed little from the times during the Vietnam or Korean War era, where children were used as human shields or bomb carriers in similar manners.

All scenarios will cry out to the American people, and many will help; however, too many have taken the precedence over legal American children and families are being burdened financially with higher and higher taxation to afford the overabundance of subsidies being paid by the government to care for those here illegally. So many must go without or have their children go without for the sake of others. The continuous sacrifice is what has become a breaking point for millions. DACA is seen as a slap in the face to many who can barely afford basic daily necessities or to send their children to college, many paying their tuition through student loans for many years while those here illegally along with their families are afforded free or subsidized, housing, medical, food, and educational assistance. When you keep cutting back and start taking away your dreams and the dreams of your children because you are forced to care for another, it is the time to say, no more and no more is what millions are saying.

As many children are used as ploys to gain access to the United States via the southern border, some have a biological connection to those who bring them; others do not. Some cross the border illegally and not at the point of entry with children, only to drop them, running away, leaving the child behind for fear of detention by border control officers. Some children are sold to traffickers, only to meet no asylum but indentured servitude.

Propagandist American politicians and claimed immigration freedom groups are seen to be no better than those who monopolize on the use of children to push an agenda. We hear of children separated at the border from their parents when the validity of a biological connection is unknown or disproven. These very groups who advocate for the children will push for reunification, and that unification may be to an unknown person to the child or worse a child trafficker. Children are vulnerable and must be protected, the protection lies within the contributing factors to each case and cannot be blanketed by propaganda play, or a political agenda yet does and has throughout history.

We are being inundated with the family separations at the border, propagated by the talking head politicians and opinion biased media that the Trump administration is evil and racist, causing undue harm, stealing babies away from their parents as they sleep, placing children in dog cages.

The fact remains that those who made the long haul to the border put these children in danger the entire way. If all individuals had entered through a legal point of entry, had their paperwork in order, and proven documentation, they could have remained as an alleged family unit. Many who are separated enter illegally through a weak border section, have no documentation, and lack in the cause for asylum.

What so many on social media who defend these alleged asylum seekers fail to realize that asylum is to be taken in the next bordering country reached, therefore that would be Mexico. However, Mexico in previous years didn't want them or could afford them, so they push them along to the United States. In 2018, under new leadership, Mexico offered thousands of migrants in the traveling caravan, jobs, housing, and subsidized income, which was turned down or outright refused by many who opted to continue to the land of plenty more, the United States. As the international agreement guidelines set forth for those claiming asylum are specific, are these alleged asylum seekers now in fear of persecution from Mexico because the terms offered were less than desirable, and they must continue to the next bordering country, which is the U.S.?

The claims for asylum are abundant, and our immigration laws have many loopholes, coupled with an overburdened justice system, a lengthy determination date is more often given, and the unvetted, unverified group is released into the United States with a promise to appear, disappearing into society. Are they justified or disgraceful? Racist or double-standard?

The numbers are in the millions of those who are in the United States illegally or termed undocumented. We hear of family separations, those who have been in the U.S. for years, now up for deportation, as if it is something new when it is not and has been done for decades, once the individuals have been detained. Sanctuary cities and states circumvent the legalities of our federal immigration laws sheltering those who have failed to follow the requirements to remain in this country are of growing concern to millions. Activists will argue that these people pay taxes just like everyone else, do not receive any handouts, are good people, and have been made to think it is all Trump's fault and the fault of his base supporters that these harmless people are being told to leave. A simple fact omitted to those misinformed by the propagandists is that an undocumented or illegal alien may pay sales tax on purchases within the state they reside in. However, if they have no social security number and their employer does not collect federal taxes from their pay, or they work under the table, they do not pay into the national system that affords their subsidized housing, education, healthcare for them and their dependent children. If an undocumented or illegal alien does have federal or state taxes withheld from their pay, it should be a concern to those who advocate for these individuals, where futuristically they will have little to no ability to collect these paid funds as SS or SSDI or the business that withheld those funds has potentially pocketed the funds instead.

States receive federal subsidies based upon each states' need reported. Anyone who seriously thinks every statistic calculated by a state is for natural born, documented, or legal citizens is sadly misinformed. In our state of Connecticut, many go without healthcare coverage for the lack of affordability, while illegal aliens are afforded free state-funded healthcare that is reimbursed by the federal government. Some are saddled with student loan debt or didn't attend higher education at all, while our previous governor, Dannel Malloy, signed a bill in April 2018 taking effect in; January 2020, allowing undocumented DACA to partake in funding for higher education funds initially intended for citizens only.

The terminology changed in the meaning of a "citizen" is another twist to our vocabulary. Once you step on U.S. soil, you are considered a citizen with legal rights to representation, civil rights backed by the ACLU, living expenses, healthcare, and free education. No longer is a citizen designated by the state or country one lives in, was born into, or that one took an oath of naturalization to a specific country, it is "just because." And that "just because" is more of a political talking point to capture the vote. Laws have been circumvented, altered in meaning, or changed to suit in a states' separate constitutional verbiage, disallowing the adherence to the very Constitution of the United States.

We have the long-standing creation of sanctuary cities and states, where protection from border control or ICE is obtained through systemic notifications or individual nondisclosure. You can be a murderer, multi-time deportee, illegal alien, and be allowed to infiltrate back into society released from custody by sanctuary policy bound local law enforcement agencies. Millions of legal immigrants and natural-born citizens are feeling the pressure of inaction, failures to provide safety, and financial burdens. They cannot nor wish to endure anymore.

When the Democrats of today speak of open arms, open border policies, it angers millions. When the State of California refuses the citizenship status question of the federal census form, millions ask "why?". Millions are offended by the false narrative that illegal aliens are considered citizens of the U.S., with the same rights as they have, including the newly instituted right to vote in special elections. Since the 1950's the federal census form has been distributed and evaluated every ten years. This census form has taken on many variations with questions dominant to the changing economic and social times. The citizenship question can be seen present on all questionnaires except in 2010, during the Obama administration, and only now during the Trump administration has this simple question come under such determined scrutiny predominantly democrat run states like California along with civil rights advocates citing this question is a violation of privacy. These very lobbyists will protect and provide sanctuary to an illegal or undocumented criminal murderer who provided our society with another angel family or was known to be a child trafficker. Those same lobbyists will hypocritically condemn a U.S. citizen, child molester requiring their whereabouts identified and monitored, or the maximum sentence for a one-time DUI offender guilty of involuntary manslaughter, of whom is also a legal citizen.

Most are tired of higher taxes paid due to the overabundant government subsidies being paid out, along with dictated government frivolous spending and forced single-payer insurance known as the ACA or Obamacare. The ACA or termed salvation to a small percentage of the population became the backbreaking financial burden for many millions more. Those millions more who were now forced to pay 3 to 4 times an increase on their insurance premiums, to accommodate others who did not fairly on the same platform of coverage. Insurance premiums skyrocketed with higher deductibles; people were being forced to choose between their mortgage payment or their health insurance. The scam was the lack of information given to those who owned property and accepted the federal healthcare plan, not knowing that they could potentially have a lien placed on their homes by taking this subsidized funding or expanded Medicaid while on this program. Others who opted out due to cost were faced with an unconstitutional fine when they filed their taxes if they didn't participate for one reason or another, therefore getting less back as a federal tax refund or no refund at all. Tax dollars that many relied upon in the heavily burdened economy that we were in, perhaps paying off that high credit card, fixing their car, or maybe making some necessary household repairs.

What appears to be a broad consensus, most Trump supporters or the silent majority gravitated to the pied piper named; Donald J Trump, who spoke directly to the hearts of the American people, understood their concerns and valued what America was built upon, not what it had become. Supporters of Trump come from all backgrounds, races, religious beliefs, nationalities, and educational foundations. Not one of them are uneducated, undereducated, or stupidly moronic as they have been called or portrayed as by some media and political talking heads, acquaintances with opposing political views, or those faceless commenters on social media outlets.

In general, most Americans wish for the "Pledge of Allegiance" to be taught and recited in the classrooms once removed, again with "one nation under God" to be inclusive, followed by a moment of silence to honor those lost protecting our freedoms. History must be taught again, and this being United States American history, how America was founded, the wishes, dreams, and advancements of those who emigrated to America, became citizens and worked hard to build this country.

Our children should learn of those immigrants who saved and struggled to migrate to the United States, how they went through the naturalization process, the element of pride that they felt when they took their oath of allegiance to their new country. Many of us learned of our family's trials and tribulations when they made that anxiously awaited travel to the country worked hard and made a life for all of us to thrive in today. Unfortunately, if these stories are not carried down through the generations and kept alive, they will be lost, inevitably forgotten.

The majority of those I spoke with who were Trump supporters are hardworking, proud people who do not wish to be taken care of by government handouts or subsidies. They want to work, provide for themselves, aspire, and achieve financial stability without having to support those who wish not to work. Some supporters conveyed that they were barely able to afford the daily necessities due to lack of work, or who had been previously employed as factory workers, who now could not find jobs in their areas, factories closed, because so much is made overseas, and the products they had once manufactured were not "made in the USA" any longer. How many times do you look at the label and see, made in China, India, Sri Lanka, or somewhere other than the USA? Every American wants fair pay for everyone, male or female, and this being a wage that allows them to save for that financial independence goal, afford their current living expenses, put themselves or children through college, most of all provide for a less financially burdensome daily life.

Those naturalized immigrants want the fairness and laws that they diligently followed upheld for everyone. They are tired of being led, lied to, and taken advantage of by rhetoric spewing politicians who have their agendas, forgetting about the roots and needs of their constituents.

Healthcare is a concern for everyone, especially as we all get older and are living longer. So many of those that supported and still support Trump was financially burdened by what was alleged to be the affordable healthcare fiasco put into place by former President Obama. This very healthcare plan, which provided expanded Medicaid payments to millions, caused a loss to millions more who no longer could afford medical insurance, choosing to go without medical coverage.

The democrat propagandist remarks have remained the same since the onset of this ACA, that if it is repealed or replaced in any way, it will mean widespread death to the nation. The very ACA plan that is pushed on the American people was the very plan the preaching politicians opted out of participating in, keeping their government-provided insurance or better stated, taxpayer-funded program. The financial hardship is one that my family knows of firsthand, and I can empathize with those that face the uncertainties. Candidate, now president Trump, ran on the promise of healthcare options, the right options, and choices that were taken away by the ACA mandate. Even though it has been stated numerous times and not changed the Democrat obstructionists will still claim any change will force those with pre-existing conditions to lose healthcare, which the opposite is exact if the parties work together and require the continual coverage, making it a law for insurance providers to abide.

Many Americans were seeing their country being run poorly by what had become what our founding fathers did not intend for; however, they had the foresight to make accommodations for; "big government." We as a nation began to lose our freedoms and control of our daily lives, being told what to eat, what not to eat, how to live, how to think, what to do, what not to do, who to like, who to accept. Requirements were being forced to take contradiction to our Christian beliefs, no longer say what we believe in, unable to stand for our constitutional rights. Slowly over the past couple of decades, our government began to act as parents to us, as their possible children, unable to think for ourselves, or survive without their guidance and oversight. By perception, we were fast becoming a socialist dictatorship, less of a democracy. The backbones of the people were no longer able, nor were they willing to tolerate any more weight. Hence millions stood up voting against the typical lifetime politician and opted the unfiltered outsider with no adherence to the politically correct culture that also had become the new unwanted norm.

Over the years, we have seen our religious beliefs or foundation of Christianity chipped away. I have seen churches abandoned, torn down, forfeited to another use. Perhaps we as a nation became too busy trying to keep up with our daily financial needs that the very moral foundation that we were taught as children were unintentionally forgotten. Our country was founded with the morality learned through the teachings of Christianity, only to have those very morals criticized, ridiculed, or condemned. Although our system was set up to provide for a separation of church and state, we have found ourselves in a constant battle for these foundational religious beliefs when it comes to the societal changes of today, where another viewpoint or contradiction challenge the infringement upon ones' Christian morality to that very same taught morality.

Those with strong convictions supported Trump, even with his questionable infidelities, as he still believed in God as being the higher power of all humankind. Donald J Trump thought that you should be able to believe and practice your religion freely, with radicalization not being a party to it. So many call Christianity based religions hypocritical, at best, because they do not outwardly condemn some of the actions of then-candidate now president Trump. What so many critics fail to realize, it is not our duty or right to judge another's shortcomings, that is left up to our faith believed creator; God.

It is not the right of another to condemn the beliefs of another, nor is it their right to suppress; this is obviously where common ground and respect must take precedence. As with the baker versus the same sex-couple, both could have been considered right and wrong based upon the view of either side. The baker had his strong Christian belief and could not accept the union or marriage of the same-sex couple, therefore, refused services for this deemed sacred event, that was very strong to his beliefs that marriage is between a man and a woman as God intended it. The same-sex couple, being joined by acceptance of the new societal norm, were offended, failing to see the religious beliefs and convictions of the baker, therefore, attempted to force the baker to comply with them.

As with many challenges, the justice system was utilized to push an event or circumstance to change, and in this case, with the baker and the couple, this event eventually made its' way to the United States Supreme Court. The Supreme Court ruled in favor of the baker, basing their ruling on the infringement by the same-sex couple on the religious freedom of the baker, which sparked considerable debate. Although many in the LGBTQ and ally groups, collectively felt that they were unjustly represented, they must all understand the teachings of Christianity do not accommodate same-sex unions nor seen as holy matrimony. God created man and woman so that they may be joined and procreate; there is no footnote to artificial insemination or petri dish embryo creations. The baker did make birthday and social event creations for these individuals; however, he could not bring himself to partake in this one very sacred event to him. The same-sex couple should have respected him and went elsewhere without the attempt at forcing him to go against his religious convictions.

The typical Trump supporter or American citizen does not like being forced or controlled. They do not wish to be dictated to, put down, condemned, ridiculed, nor spoken to condescendingly. Americans have dreams, values, firm beliefs of patriotism, love of God, and their country. They will fight and defend themselves, holding fast to their freedoms given to them by our founding fathers, bound by our constitution. When Americans feel they are being taken advantage of, they will dig in, stand firm, and fight against those that are taking advantage of them, or attempting to restrict their rights. Americans are patriots, willing to fight for others and their freedoms when necessary, they are not racist by nature, bigoted, nor do they believe they are supreme, or above any other human being.

Ultimately it comes down to a simple fact that we are all human beings. Babies are born, they become children who know of no race, color, religion, or hatred. A child will play with another child regardless of any place in society, financial status, educational location, whether they live in a house, in an apartment, a trailer, or on the street. Until a child is influenced otherwise, the child does not hate, nor can they propagate hatred toward another. Children care not whether they are a boy or girl, just that they play, get dirty, enjoy the fascinations and imaginations of each other. If we as adults could only stop and think back to a simpler time as children, no cares, no hate, and push past what we have been told to do; we would all be much better off, live peacefully, and coexist as we were all meant to do. Such a simple concept but so hard to achieve.

FREEDOM OF SPEECH

At what point did we lose track of the meaning of "freedom of speech" and cross the line of insensitivity and disrespect? A question that I have searched for the answer. Another issue that has been raised during this rather unprecedented presidential election process, beyond and throughout the PC movement.

Since the election of Donald J Trump to the White House, there has been an unhinged insanity that has evolved before us, freedom of speech is seen as the right to cause undue harm to another, burn cars, cause extensive property damage, throw items at and spit on people, injuring others to the point of almost death, causing absolute chaos. These actions are fueled by the accelerant known as the opinion media and propagandist political talking heads, the same media commentators and politicians that are supposed to be providing the American people with factual, unbiased reporting of events, so that their viewers or readers may know what is going on the in the world around them. Sadly, many media outlets are filled with opinions, bias, and propaganda, causing division and false narratives. When those false narratives are refuted, the previous storyline is quickly changed to suit the outcome, causing even more confusion in hopes that the initial fictitious story details have been forgotten.

President Trump has consistently called out the media as a candidate than as the president with the press taking offense, rightfully so, however, they always fail to realize their shortcomings and why they are being called out. If you are regularly criticized for a specified action, your ratings are falling, millions of Americans are polled stating that they don't have faith nor believe you, would you not look within and wonder why? Unless the reality is you do know why and don't care.

I have watched congressional hearings, daily White House press briefings, and listened to presidential speeches, subsequently turning to the media channels, where the narrative is, in many cases, the opposite of what was said, generally with an added twist of opinion and negative comment. In my opinion, MSNBC is the worst of the media outlets, rarely have I heard any positive to the current economy or happenings for the good of the American people. Their video presentations of speeches are a cut n' paste snip-it, without the full comment or narrative before or after, thus causing an unclear presentation to the viewers. Media heads on MSNBC, fail the American viewer significantly with their opinionated bias, causing the viewer to harbor negativity, fear, and undue emotional stress in most cases. If you prefer doom and gloom, coupled with an overabundance of drama, tune into this media outlet as you will find it regularly without missing a beat.

What became fascinating to me as I began researching this subject, was the ranking of the Rachel Maddow Show, where she is rarely informed fully, sensationalizes an issue to death offering her own opinion to the camera and the viewers within asking questions as if they were right there with her answering in a psychologically suggestive format. Perhaps as she is speaking to the camera, these drama junkies feel she is their trusted friend sitting in their living rooms. One would think after her "big news, tax form" fiasco, she would have lost some credibility; however, she did not, just a few days off, while the backlash settled down.

The secondary news outlet, CNN, tends to walk the fence, depending upon the current narrative or need for sensationalism. The commentators or alleged journalists on this news outlet offer their negativity as well; however, it will, on occasion, provide some positive happenings across the nation or around the world. The viewers of this media outlet stand a better chance at reading between the lines, providing they do get out into the public setting to see what is going on around them. Wolf Blitzer and Anderson Cooper used to be favorites of mine; however, they have dramatically fallen from grace with their biased opinion and more times than none, adverse reporting failing the positive, even for a momentary glance. Jim Acosta, of CNN, has never been too impressive, quite hypocritical at best and as of late, more of an argumentative, whining cry baby who is upset that he does not get his way or answer desired. Given the opportunity, both CNN and MSNBC media outlets will jump at even the slightest of a misspoken word, twisting it to mean far more than it does, to cause doubt to the American viewer or those worldwide.

Although many may agree to disagree, FOX does tend to report both positives and negatives, allowing the viewer to make their own decision of belief. With less propaganda play than the other networks, you can see that there isn't as much doom and gloom as reported by MSNBC, or find subjects reported in their entirety unlike the minute mention by CNN. With the seasoned reporting journalists on FOX, you are sure to get a concise history lesson that is comparative to the current events, or historical statistics and data recited consistently, and at times with obnoxious repetition by Sean Hannity. Laura Ingraham, being from my home state of Connecticut, is a hip shooter who says what she means, whether you like it or not, finding herself in a moment of a partial walk back because someone was too thin-skinned to handle her comment. Overall, I have found the Fox Network to be what they say they are; fair and balanced in this current political atmosphere. I have not seen the over the top inciteful rhetoric that is found with those reporting on MSNBC or CNN.

When the president calls out a news organization as being; "fake news," they have been proven as such with their failure to be a representative of the truth in reporting whether they agree or not. There is a great responsibility given to journalists and media outlets to report and characterize events fairly and accurately, without bias and opinion. When these outlets and individuals fail to do as such, they become propagandists and, eventually, enemies of the American people. Those who promote media play on words and comments become no better than those propagandist politicians or protesters in the streets that promote fear, violence, and hatred in a fascist manner causing division among our society.

Freedom of speech is a given right to all American citizens, written by our founding fathers, noted as the First Amendment. Written as such; Congress shall make no law respecting an establishment of religion, or prohibiting the free exercise thereof; or abridging the freedom of speech, or of the press, or the right of people peaceably to assemble and to petition the Government for a redress of grievances. This passage coupled with the preamble to the Declaration of Independence whereas; We hold these truths to be self-evident, that all men are created equal, that they are endowed by their creator with certain unalienable Rights, that among these are Life, Liberty and the pursuit of Happiness. You would think this paragraph of simple text and meaning, however, taken out of context at every turn.

The media is not just the only areas of first amendment abuses; elected officials tapping into the new form of contact are on social media outlets like Twitter, Facebook, or Instagram. Most, just like our president, find Twitter as a primary platform to notify millions of their plans, daily events, views, and or opinions. As viewers direct as it is, it can also be a dangerously divisive locale for many. A verified politician can push their views and propaganda with a single tweet. In turn, the faceless finger movements of others tweet back their understanding, agreements or disagreements, entering into rebuttal after rebuttal, some turning to threats or name-calling with the rare occasion of an agreement to disagree and move on from the subject. Being almost a popularity contest for some, if one or the other has few or fewer followers, you are ridiculed for having so little, as if it is to be taken as an insult or condescension, therefore invalidating an opinion. A good part of social media is that you can call out a politician who tweets their views or agenda with contradiction, so long as the disagreement does not incite a threat to do them bodily harm, of course.

With the overabundance of negative versus positive tweets to any subject matter, those tweeted negatives are most concerning and tend to lean Democrat or against the GOP. A simple click on the photo presented next to the Twitter screen name, you can view a quick profile narrative listed by the tweeter, giving a brief clue of whether you are dealing with a #resist or a #MAGA individual, their location and perhaps an insight of their age group. I have asked numerous individuals what they are, "actually resisting," never getting an answer but diversion or omission as I am counter-tweeted with my lack of education, stupidity, or bigotry effortlessly to avoid the answer or to deflect, ultimately ended with vulgarity and subsequent user blockage not affording a rebuttal. Rather spineless and childlike.

I consistently call out our current senators, Chris Murphy (D) and Richard Blumenthal (D), regularly for their hypocrisies, and now find many others are of the same thought toward them as well, not just being here in my home state of Connecticut but across the nation. Both, of these mentioned senators, including other elected or retired officials, find it necessary to propagate their divisive rhetoric on the MSNBC or CNN platform, many a time grandstanding in their effort to thwart the views of the average viewer away from common sense. Maxine Waters (D) of California, consistently seeks to utilize her position of political power to call for push backs, protests, and assemblies with dangerous rhetoric that can be easily misconstrued and lead to a potentially violent outcome.

In general, the democrat party of today is a whirlwind of propaganda and hypocrisy misleading millions. Those politicians that are grandstanding with divisive rhetoric are those that are dividing and destroying the country. When politicians work against the people or misguide, they must be voted out of office. However, with the voting laws rapidly changing from state to state, the once sacred constitutional right to vote for United States American citizens is being redesigned to allow illegal aliens or illegal immigrants these rights to vote as well. Therefore, the platform of the democrat party is that of identity politics.

The campaign platforms of yesterday that were geared toward safety, financial stability and the American dream are now replaced with fear-mongering, misleading the voter in belief that if you don't vote democrat you will lose all your rights, choices, societal advancements, and subsidies, this is over the top on the Democrat campaign trail. What those in the democrat constituency fail to see are those very politicians spewing divisive fear-filled rhetoric are the same who have and wish to remain in control at the cost of your rights to freedom. Those that seek to propagate hate and division do so not only by way of political rhetoric or campaign platform but that of everyday life decisions of the people, keeping the oppressed enabled beyond the ability to break free from the bare minimum day to day survival.

Governmental subsidies or societal handouts are a form of enslavement where many of those who are within the identity campaign sights have become used by the welfare system. Another identity platform is the targeted millennial population that wants something for nothing or by the effects of the high cost of living are unable to branch out on their own; therefore, the probable promise of free college, free healthcare for all is appealing. Many who fall to the campaign promises find themselves, still enslaved to the welfare system, not advancing in their lives, or again asking when will the change happen that was promised so many years ago. When the "when" question is asked, the answer from the promising politician is to pass the blame onto the other party. For these promising new era democrats is their Republican counterparts. The Republican party is not without false promises or propaganda either; however, as of late, they are far too lax in legislative efforts to be considered entirely for the benefit of the American people. With every election cycle, we, the American constituency, are met with or inundated with mud-slinging slander, false narratives, or half-truths; if you hadn't paid attention, you are at a deficit knowing where the truth lies or who lies about the truth.

Lately, the campaign trails have never left the stage of deception, hypocrisy, false narratives, and misleading rhetoric. This so-called resistance movement has become dangerously close to a civil war between the left and the right, all based on the freedom of speech and right to protest. With the media and political talking heads pushing their backward moving agenda offering validation to extremist groups the likes of Antifa, which claims itself to be anti-fascist however promoting fascism through their actions hiding behind their masks of anonymity in a terrorist fashion we see what is prioritized by the journalists as positive for America. Although they were deemed as a domestic terrorist as a group, they have yet to face charges for the such with no example being set positive or negative.

Candace Owens, a well educated, well versed young black woman, was attacked in public by those claiming to be against white supremacy. However, all those presented via video were Caucasian, shouting, and throwing objects at a young black woman; the irony is astounding. The video of this encounter was posted with an individual pointing a bullhorn in the face of this young woman, invading her space no different than that of a bully. The strength of this young woman prevailed, even though her lunch was interrupted, and the protestor bullies achieved their internet fame and hypocritical push back. The sheer foolishness, thwarted thought patterns, and hypocrisies of many of these protesters has been fueled by the condemnation failures of political talking heads, opinion biased media journalists and extremist ideologies of educators, all hiding behind the presumptive interpretation of the first amendment never once calling out this idealistically dangerous group. The argument can be that we are given a right to free speech voicing our views in opposition, the fact remains it does not hold validity to unnecessary harm or violence toward another on any level of interpretation presumed or otherwise.

The irony of those who protest today is not protesting for change like those of the past with the right to vote for blacks and women or the desegregation of our schools and society many years past the civil war. So many protesters are protesting against something that hasn't even happened, or they presume it will occur because they have been led to believe they will lose something, what that actual something is many do not even know when asked. For example, the "women's right to choose" is an issue at the forefront of the political play, where even the appointment of another conservative constitutionalist to the supreme court bench is a threat to overturn Roe v. Wade.

What can be historically viewed as political injustice, or dog and pony show, are those events surrounding the Brett Kavanaugh supreme court justice confirmation hearings, where multiple Democrats took this platform to grandstand in a way that we have not seen since the appointment hearings surrounding Justice Clarence Thomas back in 1991. Although Justice Kavanaugh was ultimately appointed, it was not without trial and tribulation; he alone could not single-handedly overturn the ruling. However, the liberal left was brainwashed to believe he could. The slightest omission of truth by media and politicians to their viewers and constituents was if there were any likely changes to the Roe v. Wade ruling, the choice of a woman's right to an abortion would fall back to the individual states.

Nonetheless, the seed of confusing misinformation had been planted; thus, the sour fruit hung on the tree. Even the pro-life, pro-abortion debate has its platform. One side of the discussion, the pro-choice populous feel it is a human right to an abortion, it is a woman's health choice, and believe funding by the government should not be in question. The opposing side or pro-life populous does not wish to have tax dollars utilized to abort a fetus just because as it is viewed as negligent, in some instances infanticide or that abortion should not be in the place of precautionary measures.

The introduction and passage of the heartbeat bill, passed in Ohio, Georgia, and Missouri, came into effect, therefore placing abortion of a viable fetus on the manslaughter or murder stage of penalties. The current political platform sparks this debate with instilling fear into the minds of those who are pro-abortion making them think that they will lose their rights when they do not, just the loss of the free ride funding to correct or eliminate what they don't want, and that being an unwanted child.

Hillary Clinton continues to intensify this pro-choice rhetoric in her never-ending poor me tour. The same Hillary Clinton that feels an unborn child is not a person with rights, viable or not, however as a contradiction to this another who murders a pregnant mother should not be charged with involuntary manslaughter or murder of an unborn child, because they are insignificant right? Would Hillary support her daughter to abort her viable grandchild, just because or would she lobby to have her continue with the pregnancy even if Chelsea didn't want the child?

With the pro-choice, anti-Trump, freedom fighters in their pussy hats and vagina wardrobes, have taken what could have been a serious discussion and turned it into a show of ridiculousness, utilizing their freedom of speech by expressing themselves as the untouchable pussy. These untouchable pussies were partially in reaction to the Trump / Billy Bush hot mike incident, then further fear fueled by opposition parties that their inalienable rights as women will be stripped away by the new president-elect Trump. Those #resistance fighters consistently forget one primary fact in their plea for justice, their congressional elected officials many of whom claim they will lose right, have more control over the budgetary funding, appropriations, and legal legislation than that of the president who will finalize with a yea or nay, signature or veto.

My husband and I went for a pizza in the quaint town of Stonington, where parked in front of the eatery was a Ford pickup with just about every section of the painted surface covered with bumper stickers; NRA, Trump 2016, Trump 2020, USA, only a few among many others. This gentleman and his wife, known to those in the establishment and most likely from the area, were expressing their freedom of speech and expression in a billboard format on their vehicle. Obviously, proud of their country, viewpoints, and the job the president was doing, strong-willed patriots. They needed no bullhorn, no eggs to be thrown, no shouting, no disrespect of someone's personal space, or violent push back, just the simplicity of a slew of bumper stickers to make their point. The unfortunate part of this is that of push back upon them and potential damage being done to their vehicle if they were positioned in an alt-left locale or a highly liberal propagandized area. This freedom of expression would be considered threatening, and even though these individuals were hardly threatening in nature, they would be the utmost evil of the evil, all based upon a propagated perception to those led by divisive agenda-driven media and politicians.

Freedom of speech was guaranteed to us as a people of this nation by our founding fathers so that we could speak out against our government, vote out those who do not work well for all of us, and so that we can stand up, fight for our rights of equality, safety, and financial stability. This freedom of speech, as intended, has become a ploy, and the double-edged sword is turning our society against one another.

Politicians and lobbyist groups use whatever means possible to maintain control and power at the cost of those very freedoms we should have. The first amendment does not give anyone the right to hurt another, destroy their property, nor shut them down, insult them, incite violence, nor invade their space. As of late, respect and compromise to coexist are non-existent. Being associated, related, or supportive of an alternate idea, political party, or belief is met with violence, bullying, ridicule, and condescension by those hiding behind the implied meaning of the first amendment.

In the same scenario as the child bullied when there comes a breaking point when the child will retaliate. This breaking point has yet to be reached in a society where there will be more of a civil uprising between the extremes and those being met with a constant barrage of illogical protestors' actions will themselves retaliate more to the side of pushback violence instead of just the vote at the polls. The unfortunate aspect of this potential civil war amongst society has been media and governmentally propagated through inaccuracies, mistruths, and malicious, intentional control of a divisive, hate-filled agenda. Sad, however true to those looking unbiasedly at both sides.

When our founding fathers comprised the constitution and amendments, they had the foresight that, along with the freedom of speech, may come a time when the government no longer worked for the people. When the government becomes too large and overbearing, the people may find it necessary to overthrow the government. Hence they made the second amendment a top priority as well writing it as such; A well-regulated Militia, being necessary to the security of a free State, the right of the people to keep and bear Arms, shall not be infringed — another amendment consistently under attack by political talking heads.

With the declaration of a National Emergency at the southern border to provide additional guards and protections against excessive crossings, President Trump's announcement came with expected pushback from those second amendment resistance Democrats who have begun the threat that the next democrat president shall, or they will push for a change, coming after the 2nd amendment rights, as firearms are to be deemed a national emergency also futuristically.

The contradiction to the new democrat ploy is that the societal root problem is not the inanimate object but the conscious individual, yet the agenda democrats will firmly believe no gun no problem. Common sense thinkers, we deduce there will be bombs in pressure cookers instead or some other means used to cause mass destruction or the death of many. We have seen it time and again. This battle shall consistently be an ongoing as the psychological heartstrings are played fervently by new era control-minded politicians as they provide a newly opened incision to the once scabbed wound of those affected by gun violence, legal possession, and illegal possession. Too many times, when a gun tragedy is reported, the root psycho-societal problem is rarely addressed as the predominant underlying issue. Instead, an organization such as the NRA (National Rifle Association), or gun lobby groups, including constitutionalist politicians are to blame.

Granted, our founders wanted the general populous to be armed to defend itself with the same arms as the government, obviously never expecting the creation of the weaponry that we have today. Nonetheless, the right to bear arms is a right, and if that right is abused, you rightfully so lose that right, but this should apply to the abuser not the entirety. We are in an extreme psychosocial change where those who are protected by privacy laws, lost in a system filled with loopholes, are committing some of the most heinous atrocities with firearms, taking innocent lives. The lobbyists and propagandist politicians, primarily democrat, have millions of constituents believing that this second amendment right, the NRA, and those who believe in this right are to blame for the psychological break and violent actions of another. We are being led to believe that if we do away with the second amendment right to bear arms, all gun violence will stop, if we allow more laws to be enacted against the law-abiding citizens, it will do away with gun deaths, and if we maintain, "gun-free" zones no one will ever get shot. On the contrary, all the scenarios mentioned are historically and factually untrue as these restrictions have been implemented in parts of the country and have failed. No legislative claim or law does not address the reality of our societal changes nor mentalities of those who commit these crimes.

A common-sense approach would reveal it is not the firearm; it is the individual and the psychiatric oversight system which this individual fell prey to, was overlooked or deemed societally capable of coping daily without oversight. With the Sandy Hook, Connecticut shooting, we dealt with an individual who was ignored by the system when he became deemed a legal adult at the age of 18, played violent video games, and had a mental break. Not only did, Adam Lanza, kill multiple innocent people that day, the one of whom you rarely hear about is his mother, who he shot numerous times, but she was also his victim too. With the Parkland shooting, you had another deemed legal age young adult, lost in the system of oversight protections and ignored by local law enforcement.

Ignorance, coupled with the lack of oversight on a known, documented individual with a history of psychotic outbursts and anger control issues, appears to be the circumstantial case with Adam Lanza. Sadly, we may never know all the determining factors, and only hypothetical presumptions and determinations can be made.

Instead of our politicians using their platforms to exercise their freedom of speech and lobby together for change in legislation to the mental health oversight issues, they seek to eliminate another right of the American people showing ignorance to the underlying root problem propagated by the psychiatry of these violent acts.

We could look at the elected officials' desire to lobby for the elimination of the second amendment right as a politician's fear of governmental overthrow as intended by our founders; perhaps they are aware of how inept they are and do not see the voting out at the ballot box a real probability or have made calculated changes to vote determination to maintain indefinite control.

As with the bully, the concern therein lies the retaliation. With the consistent violent outbursts and incitements by divisive political talking heads and media outlets, the boiling point may be reached, and this second amendment may prove faulty as the society may begin to exterminate itself not overthrowing the inept government. Either way, laws can be passed, stricter regulations, or even enforcement of laws already in place, none will make a difference to those that do not abide by the law. The rhetorical propagandists will be the only holders of blame as they hide behind their first amendment right to free speech because they were those that abused that right and caused misconceptions, misinformation, and deceit.

We are supposed to be the admired leader of the "free world," setting an example of democracy. America is leading by example, showing all people have a right to control their daily lives and not run by the government or monarchy. Instead, we are increasingly becoming a young country tearing away at itself from the inside out through propaganda, fear, confusion, and backward motion over the past decade or more. If only we could return to the days of old when we were children at play, simpler times, peaceful existence in a glorious world through the eyes of an unbiased child.

THE DRAMA PRESIDENCY

This drama presidency began with an inauguration day for a propagated controversial president and one that many would remember for years to come as the most unlikely of candidates won the electoral vote, and the voice of the people was heard, literally around the world. We were still pinching ourselves, so to speak, when inauguration day came, my son Nicholas and I sat anxiously in front of the television awaiting the inauguration speech of our newly elected president, Donald J Trump of New York.

Although, from the day Donald J Trump announced his candidacy to run for president of the United States, he was met with a high level of criticism and mockery, which would only exacerbate as time moved on.

As the transfer of order began to take place filled with a routine for the leaving first family, it was far from ordinary for the new family coming in as they were not a family of politicians nor any of whom had aspired to take any office. These were everyday business people from New York or who only had contact with the political scene by way of the hands that they shook, or the check written to fund campaigns and attend elite social events. By observation, this family, although billionaires were just as down to earth and average as most, except, of course, they are worth a great deal of green.

Donald J Trump was the son of New York, born Frederick Christ Trump and Mary Anne MacLeod Trump of Tong, UK. Mother Trump became a naturalized citizen of the United States in 1942. Fred Trumps' forte was in real estate development at the time when America was still young and building rapidly. Having aspired, and kept to their roots, the Trump family was able to help many during the great depression through the ability to fund and supply a food store.

Many criticize Donald J Trump for living the privileged life; however, and although financially capable of offering much wealth and ease to his young children, he still required them to come to the construction or job sites and get their hands dirty. A practice much the same the Donald J Trump would continue with his children.

The new first lady, Melania Trump, was born Melanija Knavs (Knauss) in Novo Mesto, Slovenia, Yugoslavia, became a naturalized citizen of the United States in 2006. Having been an accomplished model, she is also fluent in English, French, Italian, German, and her native Slovene, all of which will be an asset to this administration with their interactions with other countries.

To many, this was a day that followed a long eight years was the end of an era, a new beginning filled with hope, or to some a dark day and loss. With all the other rhetoric and condemnation by the media, my son and I opted to watch MSNBC, which was narrated by Rachel Maddow, Brian Williams, and Chris Matthews. We reasoned that this news outlet, along with CNN, had been some of the most critical during this presidential race. As the day was historically filled with pomp and circumstance, our leaving president, Barack Hussein Obama, and first lady, Michele Obama was praised and mourned by the commentators. The incoming president, Donald J Trump, was ridiculously criticized for his tie is too long, the wrong color, or that he did not button his overcoat, of which these commentators felt was lacking in class and unacceptable or against protocol. Little could be said for our incoming first lady as she was dressed and presented herself with grace, mimicking that of Jackie Kennedy with absolute beauty.

The media went as far as to complain that as incoming president Trump walked up the stairs to meet with then-outgoing president Obama, Donald J Trump failed to wait for the incoming first lady to join him. Of course, they were purposefully unable to advise the viewers that she had to be let out of the presidential car and escorted by her now assigned secret service agents. All actions were not commonplace for either of the Trumps, and now their actions were dictated by those in charge of the ceremonial services.

The Obama's stood heightened on a pedestal of admiration, and the position of the Trumps was a never-ending banter of ridicule on a day that should have been accompanied by respect for our changing of the guard. Little did we all realize that this inauguration day would be the beginning of a drama play that would continue throughout this presidency, positive improvements or not.

As the newly elected president Trump made his inauguration speech, it was hope-filled and not much different than that of candidate Trump whose intentions were to push forward for change, become a respected and reliable leader on the world stage, bring back the hopes and dreams lost for the American people once again. Our new president did not sugar coat the inadequacies of our country but spoke firmly on behalf of the millions who voted him into office. So many had reached the breaking point of despair with the past few administrations and longed for real change, to some this day was the brightest day, to others the darkest day. If you genuinely believe your cup is always half empty and you think others who propagate doom and gloom for you, it is.

From a widely criticized presidential inauguration ceremony to every breath taken, every word that was spoken, and every change made, we as a country of alleged freedom to choose were going to be taking a ride on the craziest rollercoaster of our lives. With all the changes from what had become a decade of the norm on day by day, sometimes hour by hour basis, I have come to term Donald J Trump as the energizer bunny that never seems to sleep. From day one, he has been aggressively making changes and engaging every aspect of government, no matter the obstruction, resistance, or attempted roadblock. How this man has so much energy is beyond amazing and a credit to his success-driven existence throughout his life as a private citizen. Although Donald J Trump did have his share of controversies in business and his personal life, he still persevered, and this very attribute was what he brought to the table for the American people. This business known as the United States of America was on the brink of insolvency, crippled by poor deals, misappropriation of funds, and poor work ethics, it was time for a new general manager to take over the business and make it work better all around.

One of President Trump's top priorities was that of the veterans, so on August 12th, 2017, he signed an executive order for the ability of veterans to seek medical care at any facility. An executive order to save lives and prevent further illness to those who cannot obtain immediate attention at their local VA medical centers or hospitals, due to long wait times. Veterans will no longer need to wait months for their medical treatments. Living in an area with a significant military personnel presence and being an emergency medical service provider, I came across multiple insurances and instances where treatment was an issue while military members were off base or out of the area. Back during the 1980s and 1990s, the subsidized military insurance was titled Champus, later replaced by another option, and then portions of it discontinued through budgetary cuts, and our service members were being directed to the VA or base locations only, much to their detriment. Sadly, I know of many cases where care for chronically ill veterans, in need of more aggressive and urgent care waiting far too long to obtain that medical care due to overcrowding or systematically long wait times, a couple losing their battles to either cancer or preventative care too soon.

Although an executive order was signed, the congressional approval and appropriations battle continues. The Veterans Administration has its demons to deal with on the administrative end, budgetary requirements needed to be met, and accurate to the times, those obstructionist, never-trump, resistance Democrats and some Republicans are placing the lives of our military and their families on the line for the sake of an unpatriotic cause to prove a point to their constituencies, never thinking of the damage nor the outcome.

The term "nuclear option" was put on the table if confirmation hearings didn't move along a bit more efficiently when it came to the appointment of Neil Gorsuch to the vacant seat on the Supreme Court bench. As many Democrats vowed to obstruct all nominees by President Trump, it was specified that if Neil Gorsuch were not approved, the nuclear option would be instituted for his appointment. The very Democrats that were obstructing this nominee unanimously appointed him to the 10th Circuit Court of Appeals in 2006. Inevitably he was appointed, and the option was not utilized, thus saving it for another day. Oddly enough, the day may come as president Trump was afforded another supreme court justice appointment with the retirement announcement of Justice Kennedy in June of 2018. President Trump chose Brett Kavanaugh to be his next supreme court pick, one pick like all others has been met with challenge and resistance. In the same respect as Justice Gorsuch, Justice Kavanaugh was also confirmed as a lower court judge without a second thought by the very same obstructionist democrats that look to deter his appointment to the supreme court. Senators Murphy (D) and Blumenthal (D), both vowed by tweet to vote "no," even before the actual appointment hearings, pushing an obstructive agenda from the get-go. Like many other Democrats, these two senators would begin to propagate fear and false narratives to their constituency that this would be the end of every possible left-wing advancement since the beginning of time, which of course, it would not. However, when you have someone who is looked upon as being an expert or admired as an elected official, it is easy for them to thwart and convince.

In March of 2018, the hot story was all involved around yet another staffing change in the Trump White House. So, as usual, our president tweets his thoughts and changes before they are heard on the media outlets. McMasters is out, Bolton is in. Anyone who has followed the career of John Bolton would not find this an issue as we are now engaging a different form of negotiations around the world stage. Fox News, of course, did not find it too much of an issue, but switch one channel to Chris Matthews on MSNBC, and you would be worried that you must get the bunker ready as we are "all dead." I kid you not on this one or exaggerate it; this media commentator said, "we are going to war," "we are dead." And we wonder why there is such confusion. John Bolton, aka "the hawk," was according to Chris Matthews, the perceived master of destruction, our country is at another tragic circumstance, and by president Trump making this choice at the crossroad we are headed off the cliff, obviously apparent, we are all still here and not at the bottom of the cliff collectively in the afterlife.

In April of 2018, we, as a society were met with the Michael Cohen saga. Michael Cohen was Donald J Trump's private attorney for many years, and the media proclaimed, "fixer." His office, home and hotel room raided by the FBI, all over the now-infamous "Stormy Daniels." The mainstream media can't help themselves by highlighting drama or this aspect of what they call news. What can one say but, sex sells, no matter what. Meanwhile, as the American soap opera plays, there was yet another attack on Syria, but how much air time does this get, on average less than 10% on MSNBC, and a bit more on CNN. Death and destruction of lives mean less than drama play.

With the lack of ironclad evidence against either candidate Trump or any other campaign member, the Mueller team needed something, anything to show some justification for the insane amount of wasted tax dollars on the alleged Russia collusion narrative propagated shortly after the election loss of Hillary Clinton in 2016. Our attention had to be redirected to alleged infidelities, sex with a porn star instead of job creation, nuclear threats, and proven corruption within the DNC & sexual misconducts of sitting elected officials who not only committed proven offenses but misappropriated tax dollars as payoffs. Of course, little is mentioned even after insurmountable evidence had been found by the Mueller team connecting then-candidate Hillary Clinton to foreign operatives because the actual target is the seated president, elected by the people, those same people who were underestimated.

Congressman Lieu (D) on the judiciary committee stated, "America rule of law," "no one is above the law." Well, then why was and is Hillary Clinton? Fascinating as it may be, the rule of law only applied to those who are seated across the table, unwilling to follow the grain of what has been commonly known as the deep state. Promises, Promises. How many times have we all heard this from the political talking heads only to be disappointed or reconfirmed that they mean nothing? In May of 2018 and yet another candidate turned president promise kept. Generally, speaking when a politician opens their mouth with a promise you know that the old saying, "promises are made to be broken," always stands when it is from a political talking head, especially during an election period. May 14th in 2018, marked yet another historic day in the Trump administration. After 12 presidencies, 70 years, multiple promises made, the US Embassy was finally moved to Jerusalem. Not without protest or condemnation, although hypocritical, those who are against this move were supportive in the past. As Jared Kushner spoke at the ceremony, we learned that his grandparents were Holocaust survivors. Therefore it was understandable that this would mean much more to him than many of us looking on. Ivanka Trump spoke in her fathers' place with expected grace. With an administration accused of being antisemitic, the religious diversity and beliefs in religious freedoms are proven contradictory to the accusers regularly.

With the excellent & positive motions there are negatives and on May 18th, 2018 the United States endured yet another school shooting, this time in Santa Fe Texas, where this shooter, unlike the Parkland, Sutherland Springs, and Sandy Hook shooters had no warning signs, criminal activity, psychological issues, nor was he on the FBI or local law enforcement radars. Other than a Facebook posted photo wearing a, "born to kill," t-shirt, this individual was low key. Much like the Sandy Hook shooter, this individual obtained the firearms used from his parent who possessed these firearms legally. The Shotgun and 38-caliber revolver were not high capacity firearms like the AR-15; however, this shooter succeeded in killing ten people and injuring at least ten others when reported by Governor Greg Abbott, in a news briefing. Of course, the gun control debate opened again. However, you will not hear those 2nd amendment opposers mention that this same shooter had explosive devices as well.

Meanwhile, across the globe in England, we heard all about Meghan and Harry, who now have the titles of the Duke & Duchess of Sussex, live in their newly appointed mansion with all the perks unknown to most average citizens in any country. I found myself watching losing track that I was watching reality versus a Disney Cinderella remake. America has become such a hateful nation where even so many here in the states managed to find a way to criticize this event, finding fault whereas people lined the streets in the UK days before to get a glimpse of the married couple.

With so many changes happening daily on the political scene, baby steps at best due to the obstructionism and resistance by those unwilling congressional partners, we took a turn to what appeared silly, however, relevant in some respect, and this came to be known as the Yanny versus Laurel debate. Both terms opposite of each other in phonetics but perceived differently by millions. Of course, if you do not have a written or physical view of the term, when heard, it may sound differently. Granted to the contrary of others, I heard the same as many Yanny, and nowhere near Laurel. I began to ask myself, is this the reason why we are faced with such biased opinion journalism are these individuals hearing something else, contradictory to what the rest of us heard or must you be of a different mindset to hear or see something that is not real, accurate or there?

Regardless of your perception, there is no way to misconstrue what America is experiencing; we are a divided nation with some that are free thinkers, some that are followers, others are leaders. However, the extremist is prevailing on the stage fortified by propaganda and lack of historical understanding or, in many cases, fact. Instead of embracing our past, many are choosing to erase it visually with the removal of landmarks and icons, as if removing this visual reminder may somehow change the society for good. Common sense thought would disagree as if you remove the remainder of the past, the memory will soon fade, and history shall repeat itself two-fold, which brings me to my next subject regarding history erased.

Like Louisiana, Charlottesville, Virginia, was met with an even bitter protest display on August 12, 2017. The streets filled with many different organizations, from white supremacist groups to BLM (Black Lives Matter) organizations. When you mix skin-heads, neo-nazi groups, along with those of opposing views and race, you will inevitably have a violent outburst at some point due to the volatility of the circumstances. As reported by many, the would-be protesters came armed with baseball bats and shields whether to protect themselves as aforethought or tools of action as an aggressor. Most who use the constitutional right to protest can do so, as it is their right. However, a critical aspect that our forefathers did not condone when writing this section was; so as not to cause undue harm to another, a single element that has been misconstrued and thwarted but not legally enforced unless death or serious injury occurs and even then may not be prosecutable in some courts.

The Charlottesville protest that of which should have been a peaceful debate, was not and turned tragic as a man, 20 years young opted to drive a car through the crowd of individuals, in a similarly seen terrorist fashion, injuring many and killing a young woman. Two other Virginia State Troopers were also killed when the helicopter that they were flying overhead crashed as well, although unrelated to the protester lunacy was still tragic. Even with time, this atrocity still lives with its division, nothing learned, nothing gained.

The statue of General Lee was targeted to be removed, the park renamed, and many protested the removal as an erasure of history, many saw this as a symbol of suppression, others as a loss of control or invasion of a controller upon their lives. The actual reality is that of which this statue which has stood as a symbol of the Civil War, one of which, many lives were lost in the fight for emancipation, freedom, and progression, was to be removed and no longer a reminder of those lives lost, the battle fought, nor the freedoms won. Truth be told, if you remove history from the classroom teachings, remove the symbols that have stood as reminders of tyranny, the rise up from oppression, you are destined to repeat the same in the future, preaching of fact that should not be overlooked or taken lightly.

I have interacted and studied many groups in an attempt to understand their thought patterns. One primary factor remains the majority age group of most are between the ages of 20 to 35, have been scholastically instructed utilizing the common core guidelines, know little of US American history, identify predominantly with socialist politics and world oppression without any emphasis on oppression or poverty in their backyards in America. Many of these young adults are taught to be free thinkers and stand up for themselves against anyone who thinks or believes the opposite. These very young adults have learned little to no respect for themselves and have lost sight of the fact that we as a democratic society are all supposed to be equal, however, different in thought, religion, and ethnicities, therefore, will not think the same nor have the same ideologies.

I do not agree at all with the removal or alteration of our historical symbols, and highly recommend that we get back to the basics of traditional education where the history of our country is required baseline in our schools once again. I do agree that all individuals have a right to protest; however, one that is a peaceful debate of views and not those of bigotry and hate. No protest should be organized as a white only, black, or segregated religious belief or ideology, in an effort, to divide as was put forward by the blogger; Jason Kessler, who termed this rally as a "pro-white" gathering, rhetoric such as this only puts our country backward 50 years or more.

Reverend Jesse Jackson was noted as stating this division can be attributed to the fact of Trump questioning the legal legitimacy of former President Obama's birth status as a United States-born citizen, that of which, by way of the constitution, would invalidate his presidency. To date, this question remained and was found to be questionable by other sources, but is a moot point, wouldn't you think? Questioning someone's birth does not in itself claim racism, but the legitimacy of legal status as an elected official to the highest office of the United States, would it really matter if they were any other race or creed? For argument sake, the first president to be "technically" born in the United States was our 8th president, Martin Van Buren. All others born before 1776, included are; George Washington, John Adams, Thomas Jefferson, James Madison, James Monroe, John Quincy Adams, Andrew Jackson, and William Henry Harrison, therefore the allegation can stand as far as the legitimacy of former President Obama, as it was after the founding of our country, but is not a valid talking point any longer. For the sake of a constitutional arguable point post-institution of the United States Constitution Article II, Section 1, Clause 5 sets forth three qualifications for holding the office of the presidency: be a natural-born U.S. Citizen; be at least thirty-five years old, and be a resident of the United States for at least fourteen years. Be that it may, even with the questionable doubts held in many minds upon the legitimacy of former President Obama, we must move on as his term in office and eight years are now a part of history.

MEDIA, GOOD, BAD, OR?

In retrospect, along with blatantly obvious attempts, the media is an opinion close to 75% to blame for the uprising of the exacerbated racism in this country and its connection to candidate now president, Donald J Trump, and his supporters, the balance by the #resist, obstructionist propagandist politicians. When you have media outlets consistently preaching alternative facts or opinionated renditions of truths, it inevitably causes hate, division, and discontent. Amazingly, those talking heads are supposed to be intelligent and should know the discourse they are propagating. Instead, they glory in the unrest for the sake of ratings and personal popularity.

Fascism, as defined by Merriam-Webster, is often capitalized, a political philosophy, movement, or regime (such as that of the Fascisti) that exalts nation and often race above the individual and that stands for a centralized autocratic government head by a dictatorial leader, severe economic and social regimentation, and forcible suppression of opposition.

Post-election of Donald J Trump, we as a country found ourselves amid a two-sided nation, each a towering cliff with a cavern which seemed more profound than the Grand Canyon, one slip and you were thrown to the depths of despair, or so it seemed.

Granted each president has suffered questionable reporting with an element of negativity based upon the party side of opinion, however, in this point in time president-elect Trump, his family, supporters, even those who associate or have associated at some point in their lives face intense scrutiny and are chastised just for their mere existence.

The twisted narratives caused today by our supposed truth-tellers makes you wonder about racism. With the never-ending use of the race card, should we not ask the question, is racism back, or did it ever leave? Then follow with another question, if the term fascism has a new meaning to the society, does racism as well? Perhaps if every action and everyone is racist, who or what then is not? Racism, a term coupled with hypocrite in these instances, as of late, would seem appropriate.

What a sad state our country is in one of which I have never seen before and only heard stories of from family members who lived during the racial riots of the '50s. Although we have seen many protests and riots over the past months since the 2016 election and up through the time of this writing, the one that remains as a pathetic stepping-stone to future outbreaks will be that of; August 12, 2017, in Charlottesville, VA. Granted, many other protests have followed this one, has led to violence, this ended in death much like that of the Jacksonville, FL, gamer who allegedly was an anti-Trumper, saddened by his loss at a video game tournament, opting to shoot others because of...? This divisive psychosis is what we have come to know by experience in our daily lives. Not necessarily are we met with a racial division but a social divide propagated by hatred & confusion and misinformation on both sides.

As events, social media posts, and comments follow tragic events, those in Congress, as well as media commentators, further prove the desperate need for control. And by control, I mean respect and discipline regarding one another. If we do not get a grip and reel ourselves in we will ultimately destroy our society and being such a young country by comparison to those throughout the world, what democratic example of freedom and progress do we set for others?

With the induction and implementation of the so titled "PC" culture, our country's citizens have found themselves on eggshells, afraid to speak out against what is wrong or offensive to some and a thwarted way of showing respect to others has come into play.

A comment or analogy was made to me by an older gentleman in a passing conversation; he felt that there is a switch in roles, not so much white supremacy, however the opposite black superiority or supremacy. What may hold some validity with the requests of students for their colleges to be "white free" for a day as reported by the Washington Post on May 31, 2017, where Evergreen State College in Washington, DC, demanded a "white-free" campus, which spiraled out of control whereas college professors and other students felt unsafe in their educational environment.

The point that this individual was trying to make to me was evident that many racially segregated groups one being black were presenting themselves no longer wishing to remain on equal ground with all races and creeds but want to uphold themselves to a higher standard than any other person, therefore in his opinion, they were, "black supremacists."

As I have stated before, we are getting into a hazardous area of the racial, religious, and social divide, more so than I have experienced in my lifetime. Unfortunately, as of this point, there is no absolute condemnation being brought forward by any of those who claim unity. Instead, political talking heads, media commentators, and socially segregated groups continue to preach racism, blaming it upon our current president Trump and his followers. At no point did I hear then-candidate Trump, his then running mate Mike Pence, nor any other individual of his immediate cabinet, preach nor ask for racial division. I have looked for it, listened to entire speeches, as well as attended rallies. I will only agree that then-candidate and now president-elect Trump, does at times, "not have" the societal desired politically correct filter. His comments are immediate and conscious, never meant to keep a warm and fuzzy stance with many. Therefore, every word not used in a perceived politically correct usage within the sentence is harped upon and criticized, cut, and pasted to push an altered narrative or meaning.

On the other hand, Trump's opponent, Hillary Clinton, her campaign members, and many in the Democratic party do not have the filter so as not to offend millions of Americans. We can thank candidate, Hillary Clinton, for giving millions the proud badge and title of; The Deplorables, in her never-ending condescending attitude to anyone who disagrees with her. If only someone had given this fine woman a dictionary with the meaning bold and highlighted, she would have had half a clue of the insult she stated to millions, but then again, an individual with narcissistic tendencies would not agree nor understand.

From comments such as that from Van Jones on CNN, the night of the election that the presidential win by DJT, was "a whitelash," presuming that "white" America was acting out against former President Obama, which is yet another detached comment by a media talking head. Not that the hardworking Americans of this country had enough of governmental control, high taxation, a stale economy, and being forced to provide for others while going without themselves or their families. None of this has anything to do with color, race, religion, or gender.

Candice Owens, a well versed, educated young black woman, has spoken out against the media inaccuracies and felt the backlash of misinformation herself. As she and Charlie Kirk, another conservative speaker, were shouted at and attacked while attempting to enjoy their lunch by an extremist group who shouted with at times a bull horn in her face, screaming "F%@k white supremacy. This activist group was all white, and ironically, they were shouting in the face of a black woman; perhaps they were color blind? Or better yet, they mistook her for a young Shirley Temple who once put shoe polish on her skin so that she could look black, in one of her earlier movies. Needless, to say this was yet another psycho-social moment by the extremist group. Thankfully, in this case, no one was injured.

To push the racism narrative, that of which the democrat party hangs onto during every election cycle, a most recent "black racism" narrative began to play out again. The drama our society feeds upon is astounding at times. The state of Virginia, amid a whirlwind of propagated racism where Governor Northam, a Democrat, wore a costume with a black face which was pictured in his yearbook from 1984. Governor Northam specified he was dressed up as a Michael Jackson look-a-like. This claim was picked up, and hence, the narrative was pushed that he was a racist and should be removed from office. Granted, many of us who question this new uprising against him wondered if it was an adverse effect from his comments heard via a radio interview about late-term abortion. Following the issues surrounding the governor-elect came another "me too" moment where the Virginia Lieutenant Governor, Justin Fairfax a Democrat, and ironically a black man was accused of sexual assault of two separate women. One would ask if Governor Northam was racist, mocking the black community, why would he have a black Lieutenant Governor? Next came the Virginia Attorney General, Mark Herring a Democrat, felt the need to claim that he too had portrayed himself in the past with a black-face costume.

Granted with all the drama surrounding the Democrats in Virginia, and if all were removed from office, the next appointed individual to take the place of Governor default would be a "hat choice" republican. The unique point of all of this is where the drama began and what prompted the inception of it. To the logical mind, it would not be viewed as racism nor a "me too" moment in time; it would be seen as a "cause and effect" scenario. The Republican party is pro-life whereas the democrat platform is that of pro-choice, the storylines began taking form shortly after the radio interview by Governor Northam, and after New York Governor Andrew Cuomo signed a law legalizing late-term abortion. If we look deeper and wait a bit longer, I'm sure there will be a pro-life organization or individual behind the acute onset of propagated drama in Virginia to bring doubt.

To further promote this racism narrative in our society, a shoe design worn by entertainer Katy Perry was under attack. A simple pair of strap sandals with big ruby red lips and big eyes attached were considered a "blackface" insult. Katy Perry used both big eyes and brightly colored big lips as a prop and look pretty much all the time, only now seen as an issue. Rather ludicrous, isn't it? Does it mean that she is racist? No, it does not, no more so than other entertainers who portrayed a blackface character in the past, such as; Shirley Temple, Gene Wilder, Dan Aykroyd, Joy Behar, or any of those who use the traditional Mardi Gras blackface makeup, just to name a few.

When we thought the media glorified "me too" accusation bandwagon was just about male to female heterosexual issues, we find ourselves in a fringe element of "me too," where others claim physical or verbal assault to gain recognition and keep the cynical divisiveness in motion. Jussie Smollett, an actor known for his openly gay character on the Fox series Empire, claimed an assault on his person while in Chicago. Allegedly, Smollett was attacked by two individuals, shouting racial slurs, placing a rope around his neck, hit him, and were wearing red MAGA hats. The media and propagandist politicians jump to his defense, condemning the actions, calling out Trump supporters as racist and homophobic, proudly displaying their MAGA hats, which according to all who promoted this narrative, was the badge of honor. As with most judgments passed by public opinion, moments after this accusation was announced, the Democrats circled the wagons and began their identity politics platform, battle cry while the MSM used their public view platforms preaching how the new era of Trump had caused this, while the millions of supporters were not only deplorable but disgustingly hateful. The MSM and political talking heads held so much satisfaction and outward showing of joy with reporting this negativity. What proved to the contrary were the facts that began to trickle out, and yet again, the grandstanding propaganda of divisive hatred spewed from the mouths of hypocrites slowly. When Jussie Smollett was found to have fabricated his attack, paid individuals to attack him, the same two individuals, who were to testify against Smollett who, at the time, faced felony charges and jail time. As the dust settled improprieties were found with the States Attorney Kim Foxx, who now faces scrutiny.

The media and hypocrite politicians say little by way of admission of guilt to be quick to judge, forcing a divisive narrative to the general public and the drama-hungry followers that they speak to regularly. They show no acceptance nor remorse that they, as a group, caused further hatred against others based upon lies. The media failed their viewers again by not reporting unbiased facts, nor did they as their viewers thrive on the very drama they propagate.

Where we have turned the corner, and the corner has been predetermined by those who seek to influence a new society of alleged "free thinkers." These "free thinkers" now see what is not there, hear what hasn't been said, and believe what is not real without question. A dangerous mixture when you build upon a generation that has gotten used to the thought money grows on trees, the government is supposed to take care of you, and ask you shall receive if you do not get it right away, scream, shout, demand, threaten, and destroy if necessary.

As I have mentioned, racism or the segregation of races was never a part of my educational nor familial life, nor is it today. We are all the same, in my opinion. We all have strengths and weaknesses; we all bleed red regardless of our skin pigmentation.

I have yet to meet a Trump supporter who cares about race being the end-all, or one being superior over the other. There are stereotypical attitudes toward inner cities or areas where there is a high subsidized population; however, with that, said the understanding is that the governmental structures on the state and federal levels have dictated this for decades. Many racial or societal groups are concentrated within a specific locale, much like that of the early immigration years where Irish, Italian, French, or Asian populations settled together, further populating those areas for decades to come. The sad difference between the earlier immigration population settlement times is that low-income housing and highly subsidized control areas have been designated for large populations of black and Hispanic groups, unfairly creating these environments.

Educational atmospheres and funding have been suppressed in the controlled areas and are a form of racism or enslavement to the system causing these stereotypical views. Another unfortunate aspect to these controlled areas is the use of these areas to consistently propagate hope by political talking heads, who feed on the desires and dreams of so many who are suppressed, never following through, those politicians generally being Democrats. The same party that still breeds the views of then Incumbent

Democrat, Stephen A. Douglas of whom felt that slavery should be upon the states and territories, not influenced nor changed by the government. Amazingly, still the same for those depressed areas and not necessarily all black or Hispanic, but many low- income predominantly white areas as well.

Imagine how different our society would be if Republican, Abraham Lincoln, had not defeated his Democrat opponent, Steven A. Douglas, in 1861, subsequently signing the Emancipation Proclamation in 1863, declaring those enslaved within the Confederate states forever free. You could wonder what other changes would have transpired by this courageous man if he had not been assassinated in 1865. During my interactions with others who claim racism within the Republican party or supporters of Trump, all have no knowledge or recollection of these crucial details in our country's history. Most fail to realize democrat political falsehoods have promoted the oppressive effects on their communities, more so today than any other with the new era democrat socialist or globalist views. Where does the racism lie and within whose soul is it embedded? A question we must step back from, taking a deep breath and look intently.

Republican, Secretary of Housing and Urban Development, Ben Carson, who once lived in a suppressed, low-income setting was brought up believing he could achieve anything he wanted to, took every avenue and step possible to become a highly knowledgeable Neurosurgeon, run as a presidential candidate, ultimately being appointed as the Trump Administrations Secretary of HUD. Oddly enough, his is discredited whenever possible by those who claim racism in the current White House, if this were true, this well-educated black man is seen through color-blind eyes as those who failed to see Candice Owens in the events as described in chapter fifteen.

A comment that Secretary Carson has been widely criticized for has been his comment of choice. He has been noted to imply that you need to lift yourself, move on, and attain the goals that he has is a choice; slavery is a choice; poverty is a choice. This thought pattern can hold providing the educational, governmental constraints and identity politics do not keep you back, some may disagree with this. However, you need to sit back and think about our everyday lives.

Other prominent black names; Oprah Winfrey, Condoleezza Rice, and former President Barrack Obama. All afforded opportunities not based upon their race, Oprah, in my opinion, is the significant role model and achiever in this group. You would think with all the advancements, achievements, and positives we would be beyond this era of race-baiting, we are not. The Democrat party of today consistently pushes division among races and identities, making it almost impossible to move past. Some educators are altering historical data and implanting the seeds of racism, instead of educating on the history of yesterday, with the advances of today, making it as if we are back in the days where slaves were still being transported in chains to be auctioned like cattle to work in the fields. Misguided students are protesting those inanimate statutes set as reminders of atrocities not to be committed again, toppling them, stomping on them as if killing this non-living thing in pride and success. Extremist groups are joining these misinformed individuals, further enhancing the violence and destruction, utilizing the first amendment as their platform.

Videos and commentaries of parents who place their children in shackles, making them walk in propagated shame, convincing them to feel remorse for what they were never a party to, others lobbying alongside Democrat politicians calling for reparations to those families once enslaved fill the airwaves. If we revisit our history as a developing country, compensation for one race will be blatant and inaccurate. Should we not glory in what progress was made by Abraham Lincoln, and Dr. Martin Luther King Jr., or were their efforts and all lives lost in the battle meaningless?

Regardless, we are all the same, born of our mothers and fathers into this world, not knowing who we are or what we shall become. As children, we careless of our skin color, political views, or gender, we should not care today, and should not allow anyone to change or influence us otherwise. We all can have a different opinion on how to raise our children, where to go to school, go to college, join the military, who to sleep with, who to marry. We cannot change the past, nor should we blame others today who had no hand in the choices of the past.

Another example of media bias or political propaganda play was when President Trump spoke at the FBI academy for the current years graduating class of Law Enforcement Managers, and what he stated was not what the mainstream media reported. When I began to notice numerous discrepancies, I began to listen to entire dialogues to be sure of the information, then bouncing between news channels to see the twists and turns by the opinion journalists, bewildered as to where they heard the complete opposite, of what I did.

I am always astounded when I listen to the president speak and listen to the entirety of his speech and those of others, then listen to the reporting on the same address narrating what was not there or highlighted as being, thereby, many mainstream alleged journalists. A classic example, yet again, on December 15, 2017, President Trump entertained a short media question and answer session. President Trump responded to questions from the FBI, tax bill if he would be pardoning General Flynn, to the recent conversation with a Russian regarding North Korea. You would think, okay, not a big deal right, he answered, they, the media went away to finish what should be their fair reporting to the American public, right? Wrong. Immediately, after that, MSNBC's live began their rendition of the question and answers given. Instead of highlighting the fact that there have been distinct corruption activities uncovered during the now completed and infamous Mueller investigation. Critical elements found through research that improprieties were committed within the FBI and by high ranking parties. No evident nor notable collusion at all was found linked to now President Trump nor any individual withing his campaign. However, issues were noted surrounding the Clinton campaign through the investigation.

The immediate comment at the onset of the Trump / Russia meeting, by Stephanie Ruhle of MSNBC, critically was how this president favors Russia and how the president condemned the actions of the FBI instead of supporting poor operations. She and her panel of guests this day, utterly failed their viewers as this news outlet, regularly does. For those viewers who may not have listened to the entire session, the president was in conversation with Russia primarily regarding their assistance with North Korea in conjunction with other countries such as China to improve sanctions and halt nuclear advancements.

Sadly, all MSNBC could concentrate on throughout the day is the FBI narrative, not the fact that North Korea has become nuclear-capable and has been progressing further each day to achieve their exact, unknown goal. The North Korean leader Kim Jung Un has threatened numerous locations, including Guam and the United States, which all have been determined, could be within reach of a nuclear-capable ballistic missile. The opinion-based bias media outlet concentrated solely on the Russia collusion narrative, even though after a year of wasted tax dollars, no evidence has been found. Deceptively, they as a media outlet for so many who trust in them to deliver accurate and fair reporting is doing them such an injustice.

With all said and done, should we not ask ourselves if President Trump is accurate when he makes his claims regarding fake news or that the MSM is becoming an enemy of the people? For the answer, we must judge for ourselves. If we prefer to be led then we shall follow even if truths are spoken are from false prophets, if we choose to be a leader, we shall listen carefully choosing our path based upon facts that are known and experiences had. Those media and political false prophets lead far too many, I see it in posts, and hear it in the propaganda that is relayed by others. To be a free thinker, it is not to claim a difference in opinion fed by another but different because you have made an effort to research and educate yourself to alternative facts, comprehending the meaning yourself, individually, not by an indoctrinated unified definition grouped by others to promote an agenda.

GOVERNMENT BY
TWEET OR BLOG?

I was never a formal user of twitter until this election period but became quite intrigued by the comments and feedback within the first allocated 140 characters allotted, which increased as misconceptions were evident and seemingly innocent tweets became hate-filled by the perception of the viewer unlike Facebook, where an individual with an opinion or debate point can ramble endlessly. A lengthy rebuttal can be made without too much misconception of their view on a current event. Twitter can be misconstrued due to the inability to get your point across beyond the character limit completely.

Our current president, along with many media, former and current political heads, former and present stars, find themselves in the limelight of opinion. Don't get me wrong; Facebook can be quite the same, especially the posts by Rosie O'Donnell and Michael Moore. However, the social media platform of choice appears to be Twitter or Instagram.

After setting up my Twitter account, I meandered through the aspects of following different social groups and individuals in hopes to see the wide variety of opinions and views, many there were for sure. At times I entertained or commented on some of the most absurd, specifying fact versus fiction. When I was called a bot, I questioned this at first to find out why in the world am I being referred to as a computer with programmed responses, interesting enough. Then I found that if you don't have a pretty blue checkmark by the screen name, you are technically considered unverified, therefore perceived as a bot. To become verified, you opened yourself up to providing personal information and financial data, which in our modern day of identity theft, I am not interested in doing. Regardless, I still make comments, receive tweet notifications, and insults regularly.

Once I chose to follow our president on Twitter, I found myself wondering whether this man who we elected as our president ever sleeps, if perhaps he rests for at least 4 hours a day, cat naps maybe? Guaranteed my phone screen will have a series of tweets from the president at some point by 7 am EST or somewhere during the late evening hours, dependent upon the days' events. To his credit, anyone who follows him on Twitter will know what is happening before the media announcements and reporting, as well as where he stands on the current issue of the moment.

No matter the moment in time or events of the day, our new tweeting president will announce his frustrations and boast about his successes regularly. When the media or events attack him have been portrayed inaccurately, DJT, or better known by his Twitter screen name as; @ realDonaldTrump, will tweet as many times he feels necessary to get his displeasure or point across in an attempt, to correct the misinformation or convince those in disbelief. No longer in amazement, there is an overwhelming number of those who comment on every tweet with insult and condescension, not even the slightest amount of respect. Those that choose to defend the president's position will find themselves entangled in a web of lunacy and illogical rebuttals with individuals who have so much hate they barely can comprehend why they hate; all that is known is they hate Donald Trump, as to why they cannot explain. Hence the newly titled mental illness, Trump Derangement Syndrome (TDS), and believe me, it is quite deranged at times.

Although, often a bit much, I enjoy the tweeting presidential platform. There is no mistake where President Trump stands on a subject matter, and no holds barred, if you have offended him, he will let you and the world know it, and why. I have a great deal of empathy for him and his family as they left their lavish lifestyle. The family was once going about their everyday lives with little to no criticism, now only to face what has become a second to the second insult, condemnation, critique of every word or action. Much of this current criticism is soon coming from the very people that once looked upon the Trumps with admiration and adoration, especially when the campaign check or donation was secured, leaving that all aside for the new agenda of hate. It is no wonder the president is always on the defensive.

I can still remember the day he tweeted about the transgender ban in the military. My husband and I were staying at our boat in Mystic when the daily tweet notification, "ding," was heard on my phone. I did as I had become accustomed to with this never sleeping president; "good morning Donald," out loud as I picked up my phone shortly before 9 am that morning, on it was a series of tweets which stated; "After consultation with my Generals and military experts, please be advised that the United States Government will not accept or allow...Transgender individuals to serve in any capacity in the U.S. Military. Our military must be focused on decisive and overwhelming...victory and cannot be burdened with the tremendous medical costs and disruption that transgender in the military would entail. Thank you. My first comment of the day was, "oh boy; you are gonna get some serious flack from this one, Donald." My husband asked me, "who is he pissing off today?".

This tweet sent wild shock waves into the hearts of his adversaries, and those identity play politicians began to grandstand unlike before. As I mentioned earlier, tweets can not only be misconstrued; they also pick and choose by those who want only to highlight individual sections. The debate ensued, and the rebuttals became heated. The fact remains, most who advocated for inclusion failed to understand that their forced integration was becoming problematic for many.

Under former President Obama, we began to see an increasingly disturbing gender debate happening across the country. Those who allegedly identified with a gender other than that they were born with were able to go into any bathroom they chose, enter sports designated for a specific gender group or strength category, compete and, also enter the military under a different association. Many of those I spoke to held pretty much the same view that if it is swinging, you're a man if it's not you're a woman. Rightfully so, as many men were uncomfortable going to the bathroom with what was a woman and vice versa for women. The concern also came about with opening the potential of pedophiles preying on children in the bathrooms, claiming gender identification. Lawsuits ensued, debates abounded ultimately leading to the Supreme Court where the ban was inevitably upheld, but not without societal recourse and condemnation.

On this eventful tweet day by our current President, Trump allowed me to enter into a debate with an individual on Facebook who was very outspoken on the transgender inclusion subject. This lengthy back and forth post-session became a day-long discussion. After having asked the right questions, this woman finally showed her cards and basis for her steadfast refusal to agree with the ban; her daughter allegedly was suffering from gender identification issues, she was afraid that she would take her life because it was so insufferable for her to live as the gender she was born with. This woman had consistently boasted that she worked in the medical field, finally admitting that she was a nurse for a plastic surgeon, where she was privy to many of whom wanted change or physical enhancements for themselves regularly. Although it is understandable that a mother would be worried about the well-being of her child. The underlying cause must still be address and that being her child is leading an overwhelmingly unhappy existence, who allegedly had attempted suicide, claiming it to be the cause of gender, whereas it could be another cause as the mother claimed it was not a psychological issue. We ultimately ended agreeing to disagree, and I wished her well.

My point is the same as many others if you are unhappy or unwilling to accept your God-given biological makeup to change that is up to you, not the taxpayers in America. An individual who wishes to serve their country is admirable, male, female, gay, or lesbian. It is not up to the rest of America to pay for your hormone therapy, psychiatric care, and conditioning, nor biologically altering surgery so that you can become Jane instead of Jack or vice versa. The psychology of an individual is what is in question when military leaders advocate for a "no go" on the line of transgender entry. When you enter a battle, you need to be physically and mentally capable to survive and protect those that are beside you, if you are unsure of your biological gender, it holds a question. When boot camp begins, you should reside where your biological gender falls at the time of entry, no special accommodations, no special services, the enemy will not afford you any, if captured.

A prime example of a questionable transgender person who was in the military would be that of Bradley, aka Chelsea Manning, who committed the treasonous act of conveying military information placing service members in danger, ultimately being convicted, serving time and later having the sentence commuted by then former president Obama. Granted, not all are probable to fall to the levels of Manning. The issue for forced gender identification upon others, based upon an absolute psychological need, must be held questionable and with concern that it will or may become problematic as it already is in the mindset of the conflicted individual.

From the firing of Director Comey, highlighting jobs growth, market inclines, biased media coverage, to crooked Hillary, crazy Maxine, and others, anyone who wants to know what the president is doing that day, join Twitter, he will tell you every step of the way. This president never fails to thank those in attendance at a rally, commend those in a graduating military class, honor veterans, or offer his condolences, even though a multitude of TDS individuals accompanies each tweet.

There will never be a question as to the dislike for the media by President Trump being justified or not. No matter what day, what positive event that he and his administration put forward, the mainstream media, especially MSNBC, always seems to find a way to take a negative spin and either interject the "Russia collusion conspiracy theory," or some form of negativity. The president targets CNN more so than MSNBC and this is where I will disagree with him that he is slandered more, misconstrued, taken out of context, cut and pasted to show a negative format to the viewers of MSNBC, although CNN does have a predictable habit of running a story before verification and confirmation of facts. This form of opinion journalism is failing the American public, and this biased reporting is dividing the country. The comment was made that the media had become an enemy of the people, which can be seen, as such, with the opinion biased talk show style journalism that is produced daily for the viewer.

Amazingly, it has been found that the tabloids are proving to be a bit more factual than the MSM or mainstream media outlets. The hilarious irony that to find the answers to what may be going on in the world is following suit to the movie Men in Black. As my husband and I stood in line at the local Big Y Market, we always find ourselves reading the headlines of current events from the royal couple having yet another baby to the dramas of the stars, and yes, a Kardashian is however again on the front page. Not to be taken for granted that even the once titled, "rag bags," have their moments of fabrications themselves to push a narrative of questionability.

Although much may hold to be accurate, even the tabloids cannot seem to stray far away from a petty moment. On the front page was a headline stating the First Lady Melania was changed for life and heartbroken by what she experienced when traveling to Houston, Texas, post-hurricane Harvey. Most of whom had ever experienced such tragedy and witnessed the loss of so much by so many would-be affected profoundly, and now our First Lady is human just like the rest of us, this is unheard of in the liberal world.

One would hope that this would be a pictorial story of those affected, the devastation, and the hopeful resilience of those rebuilding, along with narratives of the first couple lending a working, helping hand, playing with children, or just existing with everyone. Not at all, just beside the headshot of the first lady were two additional pictures, one of the high heels and the other of Nike sneakers. The media can't tear themselves away from any petty nitpicky aspect of their drama-filled style of reporting. On the day our president and first lady left for Houston, Texas, yes, she was wearing heels, god forbid. Once they arrived in Texas, she changed over into sneakers. How in the world is this newsworthy, and how does it help show the country any form of respect, ask for prayers and assistance? It doesn't, at all. The MSM will do whatever it takes to downplay and insult the first family at every turn, when the old saying stands, "don't throw stones if you live in a glasshouse," which many of them do.

In my lifetime and I'm sure those of you who may associate with much of what is in this book will agree, our president and his administration were on top of not only the Hurricane Harvey disaster, before, during, and after. The administration managed to multitask quite well with the following hurricane Irma, along with the spoiled man-child in North Korea. I commend this president for his resilience and innate abilities for doing what is necessary for the country despite the obstructionism and overreactive condemnation. God bless our first lady as she is also in the line of fire from those who claim bullying is a terrible thing, but yet they are the greatest and most public offenders.

Despite the name-calling, knockdowns, our president crossed party lines, and OMG, he made a deal with the Democrats? Although many say it is unheard of and how dare he, he did it and for the benefit of the American people. The debt ceiling was raised, aid was appropriated, and negotiations got done, although a unity short-lived. Trump further showed the hypocritical irony of the Democrats, and the ineptitude of the legislators, as a whole, which would come to light many times over during the first couple of years, filibusters, and shutdowns.

This may not surprise many, but within a matter of hours, Senator Nancy Pelosi was again knocking down and insulting the Trump administration even though she was a party to the deal made earlier in the day with the president. Something she vowed never to do in her hypocritical "resist" movement. Senator Chuck Schumer was and still is coming out with his glorification of the details and his party ideas or willingness to work together on this specific issue.

But wait, there's more. I'm sure fashion is yet another perceived societal divide where the rule of condemnation comes in, mainly rearing its ugly head. With style, "fads & bads," we come

To this. How many remember the new trends in how we dressed? When I was younger, it didn't matter much until I reached high school when that extraordinary Levi jeans tag was right up there with the mighty Jordache jeans made famous by Brooke Shields. Granted, you had to be a toothpick to fit into them, but it was what it was. Amazingly enough, now it matters what the first family wears more so than any other presidential family. Most first ladies were dressed by some of the up and coming or famous fashion designers in the industry costing the American taxpayer a mint for their wardrobes. From Jackie Kennedy, Barbara Bush to Michelle Obama, each first lady was credited with a specific look or flare. Our new first lady, Melania Trump, has a classic style all her own, not really requiring the assistance of anyone and can pretty much pull off any style she wishes, although she may not wear the right shoes or jacket and the media will pounce. Come on people, did anyone even remember some of the crazy outfits that our former first lady, Michelle Obama, wore? One looked like she was adorned in a toilet. How anyone could have called that fashion, I'll never know, but it must not have made an impression; it still hasn't' hit the store racks.

The first family or children were looked at but not overly stated as being in fashion or not. However, this time in our country, the media cannot hold back any negative comments but do their best to refrain from any positivity or praise. The current president and first family must consistently be on the defensive, explain themselves, only to be met with criticism for doing just that, which ends up being a "damned if you do, damned if you don't" groundhogs day moment in time for all of them.

Fashion sense is far from the top of the list of critical achievements reached in this era of presidential hatred. Just when you thought it couldn't get much crazier, Trump was, propagated as being the cause of natural disasters. The tweets, blogs, and MSM or political narratives abound with sheer lunacy. One of the many ludicrous moments of the MSM and outspoken star, Jennifer Lawrence, was when they informed the world of their dislike when president Trump no longer wished to participate in the costly Paris Climate Accord. The thought pattern was an outrage that Trump did not fully believe in the data presented regarding global warming. To go a bit further, Lawrence claimed mother nature was lashing out at him, and this is why we had such active devastation of hurricane weather. The idiocy surrounding this belief is fantastic, and it follows through on social media outlets. I found it mind-boggling that people believed this craziness when I began to see the posts and responses that followed each natural weather tragedy or event.

What is impressive is that so many can believe that weather such as this has never happened throughout history, and one man can be the sole reason for its happening. They give the president more credit than I do on this one. Do we need to look at our carbon footprints? Absolutely. Are we generally very wasteful in this country? Definitely. What many seem to forget we can throw tax dollars and billions into a rainy-day safety net fund like the climate accord or put the entire US under solar panels, stop driving cars, and yes, even put fart bags on cows, we will not halt the climate change. The US will still feel the effects of pollution. So many unrealistic people forget that the earth spins on an axis and what happens in Europe, China, and even the nuclear fallout from the North Korean missile testing eventually reaches us via the atmosphere.

Although, as of late, it was reported that the earth really isn't round, and the astronauts aren't nor ever were in outer space, so the photos sent back are fabricated. We have the new hypocritical, not very well thought through a plan called the "New Green Deal," this one has made the headlines and has fast become a swiss cheese talking point for the new era socialist democrat platform. Much like a concert tour, the creator of this flawed, New Green Deal propagates misconceptions to all those enamored by this new Democrat rock star. The narrative has changed multiple times to suit the criticisms, where the new perceived meaning is not that the world shall end in twelve years, you can still have children, but instead of global emissions control and clean energy, it is a foundation of inclusivity for all. Any time I rebuttal anyone on this, New Green Deal, I am sure to ask, "have you read it?". Generally, the argument ends abruptly, or the one claiming support has no idea of the financial detriment and lack of direction the document has.

Although ironic, one comment, Hillary Clinton, did consistently make was that "it takes a village." Yes, people, it does, however, in this instance, it takes a world. If everyone and I mean everyone changes their carbon footprint and wasteful activities, then some change will happen potentially slowing down our inevitable demise. What is utterly ridiculous are the key players such as Al Gore, of whom comments and lobbies for climate change but hypocritically have a large carbon footprint. Even former president Obama could barely justify his 9-car motorcade when touring overseas ahead of President Trump in his effort to override the new administration. Too bad, we became so smart and progressed so fast not realizing we were hurting our futures.

In today's atmosphere of social media judgments, call to action, and very way of existence, you are required to comply or be corrected, and that you shall be willing or not. When you enter in a rebuttal with another on social media, cite facts, and historical data. When you require them to fact check you, once they do, the typical response is one last sarcastic tweet, baseless, with condescension, and vulgar insult, immediately deleted after viewing, then you as a user are blocked by that same individual, no longer allowed further rebuttal. As childish as it is, you are left hanging. You can take it many ways, you were bested, victorious, irritated, or amused. Generally, the later is mine, as I do find it amusing, entirely predictable an action by many who are so critical of others in our current social climate.

For over a decade, we have found ourselves in a comply or be destroyed by suppression social atmosphere, which reminds me of an episode of; The Orville, a modern-day Star Trek version of space travel. The crew of the Orville found themselves landing on a planet in search of two previous explorers who had infiltrated this unknown world to view how the society functions. The irony that this society had a social structure based on social media for the rule of justice. Sound familiar? We are progressing or have progressed to a similar format, haven't we? With one sentence, an individual is guilty, absent of innocence or due process. A life of accomplishments can be erased and forgotten with a straightforward tweet or altered fact to fictional data done by technology.

In another time in history, the accomplishments of the Trump administration would be considered fantastical or exhilarating, not today, they are tyrannical and Armageddon. I appreciate the social media platforms of today; it allows us to read the narratives of those we elected, knowing exactly where they are coming from and view the hypocrisies that lie within their thoughts. Unlike the times of the past where we were left entirely in the dark, not knowing what an elected official really thought or how they factually voted, we get it real-time, every day, hour by hour, right from the horses' finger strokes or at times the horses' ass-strokes. A bit of sarcasm, of course, I just couldn't help that one.

The fact remains, everyone, must be diligent and more critical, concerned, and question our elected officials, more so now than any. Keep our minds open, our memories intact, and when we doubt, question, not follow as if in a routine. Just like in the fictitious episode of The Orville, they rose above the comply or be corrected methodology that the leaders of the society had put forward, in an attempt, to indoctrinate obedience, so must we, all of us who do not wish to comply with this socialistic, globalism dangerous path we were being led down.

Although the presentation may seem a conspiracy theory, we really must ask ourselves, why is there such obstruction and resistance to a president-elect? Trump's policy changes are bringing companies and jobs back to his country, requiring people able to work not be on the welfare ticket. He is pushing for all Americans to choose the healthcare program that they can afford, negotiate better trade deals with other countries that bring more capital to the country, and work towards peace through military strength instead of weakness and monetary payout? Just ask the question of yourself and others; the answer is there.

PATRIOTISM BY ANY OTHER MEANING IS RACIST?

With the NFL players taking a knee during the national anthem to the outward disapproval of how our current commander-in-chief made a condolence call, one must ask, is this social injustice or an attempt at social dominance?

No one person can deny that there is stereotyping, unfair treatment of individuals across the board, however, in the same thought pattern, you must look at all contributing factors and why an action is taken whether wrong or right.

Most should know of the "taking a knee" stance by Colin Kaepernick beginning early in the season of 2016. Kaepernick specified that he began to sit and then took a knee to show his support of what he viewed as a "social injustice" where black offenders or alleged criminals were being shot, brutalized, or wrongly accused by police officers or law enforcement. Some viewed this outward display as an act which fell under the first amendment of the constitution and was termed as "freedom of speech." Others regarded this action as a hypocritical or blatant disrespect for the country and those who fought and died for freedom.

Granted, there have been atrocities committed by some select few officers in law enforcement of whom may have acted out inappropriately, but the MSM will only highlight those that were committed by predominantly white officers interacting with mostly black perpetrators. The MSM barely will touch on or never report a black officer to the white perpetrator, black to black, white to white, Asian, Hispanic, Jewish, nor any other human to human contact other than that of which spikes the rating and causes an unnecessary uproar. The more enhanced the drama, the better the story, and many times if a story does not exist, one is enhanced or hyper-exaggerated, causing condemnation before judgment.

As my husband and I watch the daily news, never does a day go by that there hasn't been an inner-city shooting in our capital city of Hartford, Connecticut. Predominately black communities, shooting each other either in gang-related or domestic circumstances. It is beyond unacceptable and highly unfortunate that we need to even hear about killings at all. The alleged polls will tell you crime is down in some areas and up in others, but will blame social injustice, racism, or gun control.

The MSM does a fantastic job of making its viewers believe that it is all about race or a black/white issue, but how can this be accurate when the majority of city killings are black on black, gang-related or drive-by accidental casualties? Is one to believe that they are racist to each other?

A societal aspect that is blatantly apparent to anyone who stops to look around them and truly see what is going on that, yes, there is a social injustice. And the inequity stems primarily from our governmental oversight and frivolous spending, which takes away from many community support systems allowing people to advance a breakout of the ridiculous life conditions that they are in at the time. In a country that is supposed to be so advanced and considered the leader of the free world, we should have no poverty and live in unity as we have fought for over the years since our inception.

Dr. Martin Luther King, Jr. was an amazing man who trudged forward and became a pioneer in racial equality. We made so many advancements and yet here we are today so much further behind the platform of balance than we have ever been.

Growing up in Connecticut post the segregation turning point of Brown v. Board of Education, we had students of color in our school, and one of our local police department sergeants was a black man. Our local college librarian was a well-educated black woman of whom replaced another highly intelligent Asian woman and many black individuals that were an integral part of the community. Racism was a non-issue for us regardless of race, religion, gender, or otherwise. With this paragraph written I could respond to the question that I do not know of the racism that so many speak of, as my family and I were not privy to such an aspect of conditioning in our lives, hence, why I reached out to others across the nation for their views and input. I found little by way of blatant hatred for another because of their origin than those segregated few who either have not accepted change, or those who had been propagated to believe racism is a right to think, just because it works for them and the argument.

I honestly didn't experience any form of racial tension even when I traveled to Virginia to attend college. I began my studies in Connecticut, taking a couple of college courses while I was still attending high school, then continued my studies, out of state. Having worked as an Emergency Medical Technician, part-time as a grief counselor, and part-time as an intake specialist for a head trauma rehabilitation facility provided me with a view of real people in real-life experiences and the issues that surrounded them in times of crisis. We also had the HIV issues that many families were trying to cope and deal with during the '90s. Granted, in the medical field, race does come into play with certain types of diseases, and the ability to diagnose a trauma patient. And yes, a black patient is sometimes far more difficult to diagnose due to their skin pigmentation. However, that doesn't mean you are racist. Above all and in the face of any tragedy, we all bleed red, and our hearts beat until the day we die.

During the Clinton presidency, our country was faced with the threats of multiple or impending base closures, which would affect the economic structure of the Hampton Roads and the Virginia Beach area. Not one person cared about what race you were, leaned on each other, helped one another above all stood when the anthem was played and on every military base or ball field where a game was played everyone stood as one, placed their hands over their hearts and turned toward the American Flag. Never was there a question as to why we were all brought up with respect for our country. Those who died for our freedom, those who still served home and abroad, but most importantly, we all knew what our anthem and flag represented.

During previous presidencies, were there social injustices? There were improprieties towards others; however, never did I hear, watch, nor experience the blatant attempts to divide us as we are experiencing now. I do agree that everyone has the right to freedom of speech and expression as given to us by our founding fathers; however, those who protest must also understand that our founding fathers did not expect this constitutionally granted or guaranteed freedom the implied allowance to insult or hurt others. Our protest actions should never include the very symbols that represent our country.

When the schools stopped standing and teaching our children the Pledge of Allegiance, and learning what the colors woven through the fabric of our American flag represented, began the start of a backward motion in our country and enhancement of disrespect for others as well as lack of acceptance for those who think or are different than you.

Although, I got a bit off track by going down memory lane the crux of my point is that no one cared what race you were, no matter the circumstances, we seemingly had all moved past that day when bathrooms were designated, busses were categorized, and schools were white or black only. A far cry from what we are dealing with today or what is being imprinted by the opinion biased media play, and yes, I do blame the MSM for a great deal of the hypocrisy and racial divide that has come about over the past 8 or so years. One would think that with having the first black president we would be passed this issue and rejoicing in the progress our country has made since those days of segregation, but instead, we have been thrown down into the cesspool of dangerous drama play forcing so many to look at each other differently.

Some will blame former President Obama for the division; some will blame current President Trump. In actuality between the compilation of opinion politics, biased journalism, and the lack of US American history taught in our schools, how can anyone fairly judge their surroundings and be free thinkers if they have been conditioned to hate or look at another through the eyes of prejudice from the onset?

Our society is now placed itself into a vortex of hatred which is fueled by rhetoric spewing politicians of whom have their agenda along with the mainstream media and their biased fed opinions on all those who listen and admire the simplistic factor that these journalists must be highly intelligent and always right because they are on TV. How contrary to the truth this is.

I, as many others, were very offended when other NFL players began to kneel in solidarity with Colin Kaepernick. Even though Kaepernick was known to be a failed quarterback, opted to be a free agent, along with his outward expressions of insult by either taking a seat or knee during the national anthem or wearing socks depicting cops as pigs. The inability of Kaepernick to be signed to another team was on him and not by anyone else's choice. He was a free agent; he should solicit where he wishes to go. When Colin Kaepernick was not being signed to play, he took this act of defiance one step further and began to play the now-infamous use of the "race card." Now his issue was that he was a black man acting out, so no one wanted him. The absurdity is astounding. Even the NFL team coaches, owners, nor players cared whether he was black or white. When

Colin Kaepernick was not getting his opportunity to sign with another team some of his NFL colleagues across the country opted to begin to take a knee in solidarity with "whatever" Colin Kaepernick was protesting or why some did not even know, just that they were supporting one of their own. These kneeling actions inevitably proved to be financially detrimental in the long run to the NFL, which they needed to do damage control and compromise to regain their followers.

One instance which was perceived as a radial force of the hand was by coach Mike Tomlin of the Pittsburgh Steelers when he condemned Alejandro Villanueva on September 24th, 2017, for coming out of the locker room and standing for the national anthem. Many photos of this once United States Army Ranger, who served three tours in Afghanistan now an NFL offensive tackle, can be seen with him standing tall with his hand across his heart while his teammates' huddle in the locker room. Coach Tomlin, who is a man of color, came out in a press conference stating that "he thought it was understood and that they all agreed to stay in the locker room," a comment which indicates more than it says. Although coach Tomlin denies outwardly stating to the players that they will not leave the locker room, he did specify that it was discussed and the players themselves had a private get together and made their uninformed action agreement. Social media play had an absolute field day with this controversial action with some comments that were pathetically disrespectful to the players, some attacking the coach specifying that he was black and wanted to control his players, and then there were the supporters of the actions both, those that remained in the locker room and that of Villanueva. The irony of all this was that sales of sports memorabilia and player items skyrocketed for Villanueva, even after he regretfully came out in a press release saying he was sorry for not staying with his team in the belief it was all his fault.

In the weeks to come many NFL players and teams would recant their actions offering numerous apologies in hopes to regain the fan base that was so insulted and disgruntled by their actions, many of whom stopped watching games, buying sports items, burning their NFL jersey collections and turning back in their season tickets. Pointing out that unity has a price tag. Their actions hit many Americans in their hearts, so they retaliated by hitting the NFL in their most vulnerable spot, their wallets.

Colin Kaepernick, realizing that the many avenues that he had taken led him to a dead-end, he opted to sue the NFL, claiming lesser players had been signed before him. What he still fails to realize the ownership of this is upon himself; he is, after all, a free agent, so he should be his own agent, negotiate a deal. Even later, Colin Kaepernick, commented that he would stand during the anthem if he were signed, the damage had already been done. Now, most would ask, what is he trying to accomplish by backtracking? Ultimately, a monetary settlement was reached between Kaepernick and the NFL, so the accomplishment has been finalized with a windfall to Kaepernick only not his alleged and initial protest claim, which remains open without any further effort on his part.

Of course, these actions by the NFL players in conjunction with Kaepernick sparked the debate between freedom of speech or expression as a constitutional right versus the respect for our country, its military, and those who gave the ultimate sacrifice, with the loss of their lives. To fully understand the disheartening of so many millions of Americans, one must first understand and acknowledge why. Many do not know the meaning of the colors of the pales or the vertical stripes of the American flag, those of which the white signifies purity and innocence — the red stripes, hardiness, and valor. The blue background means the color of the chief, and lastly, the broad band above the stripes signifies vigilance, perseverance, and justice.

In part, to protest social injustice as Colin Kaepernick and his followers claimed was his goal, would not be far-fetched. However, it is a grey area as the symbolic representation of those who fought and died, raising our flag symbolizes progression. For many, the American flag was and is a symbol of hope for those who wish to emigrate here to the United States in search of a better life for themselves and their families.

When Buzz Aldrin saluted the first American flag erected on the moon, July 21, 1969, it was not only a testament to the intelligence of man but the will and determination, along with the respect of those who fought and died allowing that historic day. On the battlefield, the flag flew tattered and torn held by those bloodied and beaten as a symbol of strength and unity, erected at the highest point to show perseverance and the battle won.

I asked a young many if he knew what the American flag stood for and if he knew why it was draped over a soldiers' casket? This young man's response to me was that "its because he was American, that's all." There is more to God, Country and the respect for our, ever flying the American flag, and as a reminder to so many who have forgotten or did not know, this is what I responded to him. Although in part, he was correct, this fallen soldier was American. During a military funeral, the flag will be folded 13 times with meanings as specified.

- For the symbol of life.
- Belief in eternal life.
- The honor of those veterans who are departing the ranks who gave a portion or all for the defense of their country to attain peace.
- The weaker nature for as Americans it was the belief in divine guidance.
- Tribute to our country, right or wrong.
- For where the peoples' hearts lie and wish that they pledge their allegiance.
- A tribute to the Armed Forces, for it is through them that we have safety and boundaries.
- A tribute to the one who has entered the shadow of death and that they may see the light of day.
- A tribute to womanhood and mothers, for without them, their faith, love, loyalty, and devotion, the character of those men and women who have made this great country would not have been molded.
- A tribute to the fathers, for they too have given to their sons and daughters the defense of their country since they were born.
- Represents the lower portion of the seal of King David and King Solomon, further glorifying in the Hebrews eyes, the God of Abraham, Isaac, and Jacob.
- Represents the emblem of eternity and glorifies in Christian eyes, the Father, Son, and Holy Spirit.
- When the flag is completely folded, the stars are in the uppermost portion, "In God We Trust."

After the flag has been wholly tucked in it takes on the appearance of the crooked hat, reminding us of the soldiers who served under General George Washington, the sailors, the marines of whom served under Captain John Paul Jones, their comrades of the Armed Forces of the United States, preserving the rights and freedoms they all enjoy today. So many did not know of the thirteen folds, and some presumed that it represented the 13 original colonies.

Some traditions are slightly different, but all stand true that our flag is an embodiment of all of us who are Americans, those who continue to serve, will serve, have fought and died affording us all these great opportunities that so many now take for granted. That "piece of fabric" that some have called it holds our past, present, and our future as a country. Our flag shows no prejudice, condemnation, or segregation. Our banner stands for no less than perseverance, strength and should be held in the highest regard to all those souls wrapped up within it.

As I mentioned earlier, when a young man grabbed the American Flag from another individual, who was stopping on it at the Trump Rally in Hartford, Connecticut, that night, he was probably one of the most impressive actors and sights in the eyes of many, myself included. This young man was the epitome of patriotism, which brought a tear to my eye, pride, and then as I looked around a heavy heart from the display of disrespect around us all as we descended the staircase to leave that night.

ME TOO – I DON'T KNOW,
BUT YOU TOUCHED ME

Here we go again, is all I can comment to start this chapter. With the backdrop of Brave New Films, on day 3, when the alleged Trump accusers banded together for an awakening of their suppressed memories. Those lost memories of the past, whether valid by action or through presumed happening, were being set front and center for all America to believe or disbelieve. Now in our tumultuous time any female, which has been the primary accuser base thus far, can come up to the media and not only say, "me too," but can make an allegation against any male counterpart and by way of public opinion, he is guilty as accused whether fact-based or not. This slippery slope is one that we as a society should not even venture down as it will tear away at the very due process fabric that our country has been built. We are becoming the society of no longer innocent until proven guilty by judge and jury but convicted by opinion journalism and social media based on accusation alone.

Starting with Harvey Weinstein, the media and Hollywood began to circle like sharks waiting for the next live bait to sink their teeth in. After a prolonged overzealous inundation of Russian collusion and lack of validation, millions of dollars spent only to uncover past financial improprieties of Paul Manafort, deception of truth by General Michael Flynn, we have them, it was you, sexual predator, hypocrisy at all levels became abundantly evident.

As some members of the Trump campaign were now under scrutiny, incarcerated, or indicted, the narrative began to change, as the radical left was in another tailspin. Not only were the initial ideas put forth that it was the fault of Russia that Hillary Clinton lost the electorate, but now we have elites, democrat elites under the microscope of morality? When the American public thought the soap opera drama might be over, here comes Charlie Epstein, pedophile extreme, the epitome of righteousness, close acquaintance, and confidant to elites; former President Bill Clinton, Prince Andrew, and many others. The plot thickens as Epstein is curiously found allegedly hung in his jail cell. Did he really commit suicide or was it just coincidence that the cameras stopped working for that moment in time?

Epstein or Weinstein, the choice is ours to determine who was more predatory. Would any of the accusations been of pertinence if it were not for the "me too" movement? Most likely not. The hypocritical democrat elites propagated a narrative to slander Trump, in turn, placed a beacon of light upon themselves.

With the access Hollywood tape still in the shadows of everyone's mind, the stage was already set for what is now the "me too" bandwagon. It has been quite fascinating to see the consistent comments by many both on Facebook and Twitter, many of whom are still brushing the tape off, and those that claim was an absolute admission of guilt by then-candidate Trump.

The misogynistic hyperactive narrative came when candidate Hillary Clinton noted that women were not wholly veering away from her opponent and remained biased to her candidacy, thus threatening her ability to make a clean sweep of the election. These women of whom continued to support or shy away from her were deemed less than adequate later to be considered subordinate to men and were told what to do, having no mind of their own. This belief and lunacy continued and was further reiterated by former first lady Michelle Obama during a speech in September of 2017. Michelle Obama specified, "any woman that voted for Trump was a vote against their voice," or "that they were told what to do and voted for Trump." Of course, millions of free thinkers throughout America became outraged by this, and I could do no more than sit back and laugh about the entire speech. I asked myself, if a vote against Hillary Clinton was such an atrocity, did or would Michelle Obama even consider not voting for her husband Barrack in place of Hillary? Did Michelle Obama listen to her voice when she turned away from Hillary Clinton when she challenged Barrack Obama in the primaries in 2008? Oh, the hypocrisy, it is never-ending.

After Jeff Sessions was nominated and subsequently confirmed for the appointment of U.S. Attorney General, left his Senate seat open in

Alabama. Even though now president Trump supported Luther Strange as the Republican choice, his opposition supported former Judge Roy Moore to be the running candidate for the Republicans in the special election. Inevitably Luther Strange did lose this bid, and Roy Moore was chosen with his opponent being Democrat Attorney Doug Jones. With the Democrats having lost so many seats during the Obama years, it was crucial that the Democrats do whatever necessary to gain that vital seat, even if for a short amount of time until the 2018 midterm elections.

Now, although it may be deemed speculation, conveniently and out of the blue, Judge Moore had alleged skeletons sneaking out of a dark closet. Accusations against Moore began to fly, starting with Beverly Young Nelson, who came out to the public eye with the infamous Attorney Gloria Allred by her side. Ms. Nelson announced that she had been forcefully abused by Moore when he was a district attorney many years prior. Ms. Nelson alleged that Moore caused a bruising on the back of her neck and assaulted her after picking her up from her workplace when she was only 14. Conveniently, in sequential fashion as other accused men in the spotlight of power, multiple other accusers came forward to specify that they too had been inappropriately treated by Moore, thus bringing reasonable doubt to the minds of many Alabama voters. Not only were the voters affected, but it also didn't help that house majority speaker Mitch McConnell and other prominent Republicans began to jump ship calling for Moore to step aside from the election which he fervently denied allegations and refused to do.

President Trump made a tiny comment on the allegations only to state that, "if the allegations are true, he should step aside," not favoring belief or disbelief either way. Of course, no matter what the views of the president, especially being that it was Donald J Trump, it was open for immediate condemnation and scrutiny.

With Democrat Senator Conyers of California, finally stepping down after allegations tainted his history and the uncovering of what would be titled as the "hush fund," house minority leader Nancy Pelosi would be heard calling Senator Conyers an icon, only to hypocritically drawback and change to it was time for new blood in office, so to phrase.

What I and many others find hard to fathom is that Congresswoman Pelosi has been in elected office for 30 years and had served in one of the highest positions of trust in the country, had no clue nor idea there was a separate fund set aside to pay out hush money to harassment claims made against members in office. This fund was noted to have been paid out in the millions of dollars in settlement claims over the years. Obviously, taxpayer-funded, yet no one knew? Huh? Mind-blowing, isn't it?

Even now, as Congresswoman Pelosi was appointed to House Majority Speaker, she and her Democrat colleagues are still silent on this issue that should be made transparent to the taxpayers. All those who pay attention would know that once the #resist, obstructionist Democrats gained control in any form, there would be little told about any governmental improprieties, uniquely those inclusive of Democrats.

One would think with the high number of women elected to political office in 2016 and 2018; there would be a push for transparency on political wrongs done to women over the decades, to the contrary, the only drive is to remove the dually elected president from office who emits toxic masculinity.

To Conyers demise, he paid one or more of his accusers out of his congressional office budget allocation, which was a tarnish or attempt at the Democrats to save face, so he was advised more aggressively to step down from his seat after holding it for 52 years. Amazing, isn't it? Astounding, 52 years, the same amount of time many of us have been alive. All I can say is WOW, and we need term limits.

Around the same timeline, we had the Democrat Senator Al Franken saga, with his accuser, Leeann Tweeden coming forward in her "me too" moment. She made her claim, and this one came with photos. Hard for him to deny the allegation with absolute proof, he apologized. Shortly after that, multiple allegations began to come forward against Franken, and it was evident that it was going to be his time to go as well. He made his concession speech, stating, "he was sorry for making anyone uncomfortable; however, he remembered things differently," then he added a hit against the previous unsubstantiated accusations against then-candidate Trump and the current Republican candidate Moore who at that time was running for office in Alabama's open Senate seat. Pass the buck politics, or the commonly used comment on social media now is deflection.

When you thought it was "men only" accused of improprieties, here comes the opposition. Democrat Andrea Ramsey from Kansas came under scrutiny for a case of harassment settled a decade ago. When then Democrat Elizabeth Esty, from my home state of Connecticut, conveniently opted to not run for office again in the midterms, after reports of how she handled a sexual abuse office misconduct issue by one of her staffers against another in her office, offering him a substantial severance and stellar work reference when he was asked to leave.

From sexual abuse allegations decades later, the "me too" movement does the same. Many of us have had our experiences, some that cannot be spoken of, or we wish not to speak of them. As women, we face so many stages in our lives that can make or break who we become as well as, how we perceive others, men especially. Everyone has a story to tell; everyone has been in a position of discomfort by a provocative or flirtatious act, sexual advance, or inappropriate touch and violence. Some needed the strength of others, joining a group to relieve themselves of memories they wish to forget, and others, like myself, have memories long suppressed brought back to the surface, that are desired to be forgotten.

What is hard to comprehend are the allegations after decades of time, some being against those that are deceased, most after the statute of limitations for judicial conviction is passed. Many accused have been in high positions of political power or public office, and even accusers have led full lives, had families, and had become successful. What is the point of condemnation so far in the future?

With the Catholic Church abuse allegations, many receive a financial settlement, perhaps have some closure when they obtain a financial gain; however, does the trauma of the event go away can be asked. As many claim a shock so terrible decades later but never mentioned it until the probability of financial gain or political turmoil can be achieved makes even the most believable questionable to reason.

Although the "me too," pussy hat-wearing women of choice have all but settled back into the shadows of existence for one reason or another, with the perceived victory that we have created a society where men must be on the defense from puberty until death.

Having worked in the EMS field where I have been a witness to some of the worst abuse cases to cases based upon anger and self-inflicted harm by the alleged victim to cast blame on their male counterparts, I tend to err on the side of caution before jumping on the bandwagon. Although I have been a victim in the past, I do not hold all men accountable for the actions of one, nor do I feel a victim should be believed just because she or he states an accusation as truth.

If we all did as the politicians and the MSM tried to convince us to do, we would be creating more victims than curing the physiological or psychological problem of others. When the accusations are against another based upon falsehoods, like many of those in today's societal atmosphere, it is not just the accused that becomes a victim of the accusation. Social media and false judgments before validation, effects, spouses, children, family members, and could cost someone their job or years of accomplishments by public opinion alone.

On the other hand, too many accusations can lead doubt to the real victims claim. As the mother of a son, I am concerned with our society changes. The creation of the belief that women are to be believed without a doubt in an environment where men are now considered to have "toxic masculinity" makes for the question, should he have an escort, even at the age of 23?

Women have more power than they believed they had, and only in rare cases did they not have the believability or upper hand. With this new movement of accusers, the tides shall change for them as well, leading to a common ground of accusation and belief.

I have spoken to gay men who have been abused by their male counterparts, and lesbians who have suffered abuse by their female counterparts, yet neither fit within the believability of the "me too" scenario. Are they to be considered insignificant because of their sexual choice, and only a heterosexual relationship is a qualifier?

Men are seemingly being required to engage less, admire less, or become less strong in the era of the superior female. Face it, men and women are different, their psyche is different, their hormonal makeup is different. If women do not wish to be looked at adoringly or with sexual desire, they should not enhance their image, wear seductive clothing, or flirt to capture attention. Men should do the same. We all should wear the same gray tablecloth, covering head to toe, shave our heads, never touch, engage each other in any way, procreate using a petri dish, and in-vitro fertilization.

Although it seems as though I am laying condemnation to this movement, I am not entirely, however, warn of the dangers of scenario that will inevitably bite you in the ass one day as a progressive society.

LIFE INFLUENCES

We are influenced in our lives by the very experiences we have. The chance meetings, good bad or indifferent play a role in defining how we may react to a situation or circumstance in our futures. Positive or negative influences do not necessarily come from our parents or guardians but can come from the most unusual of people or places. Religious beliefs or lack thereof can play a large roll in our acceptance of viewpoints and opinions that differ significantly from ours.

Although irrelevant to some, the simple celebration or acknowledgment of Christmas came to be a political point in rebuttal by many. Presidency after presidency has followed the same tradition of acceptance of the White House Christmas tree. A tradition fulfilled by finding just the right tree with the right height and diameter to be considered the perfect tree to be adorned as "the tree" for that year and an honorable mention proudly accepted by whoever grew it.

The first Trump administration Christmas tree was delivered to the White House on November 20th, 2017, by way of a horse-drawn carriage, as has been done for decades. A beautiful tradition where the First Lady accepts the national tree chosen.

As the First Lady Melania accompanied by her son Barron, was reported and seen circling the wagon acknowledging the traditional acceptance, Facebook, Twitter, and Media outlets were all astir. Positive and negative comments, as always. Comments ranging from, "I'm so glad we can say Merry Christmas again," to the typical bah humbugs criticizing every aspect. I again found myself liking and wishing many of those whom I never met a Merry Christmas, God Bless and agreeing how wonderful this is to be another holiday season upon us in America.

The well-wishing never goes without the comment by the negative faceless internet posting Nellie who just can't find anything nice to say, so I commented to this individual that they must be a very angry person with so much unhappiness in their life, then commented that perhaps they should go outside and take a breath of fresh air it might do some good. What happened to everyone? Have they become so disgruntled at the wonders of the past are pushing their way back into our lives, causing even the slightest of joy and happiness? Could these people have had such a terrible childhood that they can't even remember how exciting it once was to lie in waiting with one eye open hoping to see a glimmer of red in the sky from Rudolph's nose?

When my son was little, he and I would go out on Christmas eve with the magical box filled with reindeer food. This box was filled with magic pixie dust, sparkles, and oats (just in case the reindeer were hungry). The box stayed closed all year long, perched upon the shelf waiting for a short time after Thanksgiving Day when the new Christmas tree would be erected in the living room where it would be placed until it was time to call the reindeer. The amazement in his young impressionable eyes when he opened that box each year to find it full again, always curious how it was so, considering it was all but empty from that last Christmas eve night tossing the magical feed into the air, calling all the reindeer by name.

As we opened the box, we each took a handful of magic and tossed it up into the air reciting; Dasher, Dancer, Prancer, Vixen, Comet, Cupid, Donner, Blitzen, and of course, Rudolph. Many a Christmas eve there was just enough snow on the ground and enough moonlight that the glitter dust or magic dust would glisten as it fell to the ground. Once the box was empty, we would run back into the house so we could get to bed quickly before Santa came, because Santa liked to be secretive. There was always milk and cookies for Santa, because it was a very long night for him, traveling all around the world delivering gifts.

How exciting it used to be when you woke up early, ran downstairs to find presents under the tree that were not there the night before. Even as we get older, there is still an unexplainable feeling that comes about during the holidays, is it magic? Perhaps just the warm memories of the past touching our souls? Or the magic of God's love and the miracle of Jesus' birth?

For far too long and sadly still valid, those that have alternative views fight to take away that same joy many of them shared with others as children. Not all Atheists, Scientologists, or those that do not celebrate the Christmas holiday were always in opposition. Their lives changed as they grew older, and their beliefs became different. As a country with a melting pot of faiths and nationalities, we were never intended to suppress another because we choose or have been brought up to believe or think otherwise.

To say Merry Christmas to another instead of the politically correct are all encompassing Happy Holidays is far from life-altering, yet some believe it was so hurtful to their very existence they could not function. With the promotion by a candidate now President Trump, the simple term, Merry Christmas, is now a new use of racism, anti-Semitic accusations dramatically flowing with opinion, when the opposite is exact. What is true are classic examples of condemnation called by activists such as Louis Farrakhan and newly elected Congresswoman, Ilhan Omar, both of which speak out against the Jewish community and their religious practices with condemnation fervently, however, justified by their anti-Trump followers or Democrat party counterparts.

Regardless, I and millions of others shall say Merry Christmas, Happy Holidays, Happy Thanksgiving, and Happy New Year, every time as we always have. I was brought up and so was my son, if the terminology is so critically offensive to another, they do not have to reciprocate by saying it back. Simple. We all shall go our separate ways continuing our lives as we had before our brief interaction in time.

From the condemnation of religious beliefs, saying Merry Christmas one month of the year, to offense taken to every perceived misuse of a word, we, as a society, have entered an unhealthy segregation from one another starting decades ago. Although I am not sure where it all began to take form and believe me, I have tried to determine the exact changing point where our society went from a peaceful attempt at coexistence to "sheer lunacy."

From the women's march, which descended upon Washington, DC after the 2017 presidential inauguration to protesting for what? Well, basically, whatever the flavor of the day is, that is the narrative of the protest. To say the least, our society has taken a sharp turn. I was brought up with the thought pattern that at some point in your life you will be standing at the crossroads, you will choose which way you will go and then again, a fork in the road where choices will need to be made yet again. How you want to follow your path in life will ultimately be your successes or failures. Seemed simple when explained to me by my grandmother and other elders in my life at that time. Now having reached the half-century point in life, I can only look back and see where I should have turned and where not to have.

Life was always to have stepping-stones, leaps, and bounds, roadblocks and detours that we learn from, become stronger, and learn from our mistakes. Granted, we did have a little help along the way from others, but for the most part, it was indeed our choices that defined us in the end. Although some may consider it biased or lacking in acceptance, I can assure anyone reading this that you have at some point found the actions of others not up to snuff or appalling in some form or fashion.

Take, for instance, the belief of how a child is raised or nurtured. Generally, a boy raised to be strong, however, still taught empathy for others. He was shown to be the rock in the foundation of a marriage, the provider for the solvency of the family. A girl was shown to be just as strong emotionally but with the more outward expression of compassion, a caregiver, and the foundation of the family in the future with her husband, further teaching their children the same. This philosophy of child-rearing commenced for generations, until now.

Eventually, women became more empowered, voicing their opinions fervently. During wartime, women had to leave the households and become the working provider as the men were at war, fighting the battles of our country and others. Independence began where the woman was now the provider, caregiver, educator, and foundation, all wrapped up in one package. Eventually, women were able to provide on their own for their own without their male counterparts.

In earlier years, the word "divorce" was unheard of as a norm in society. No matter the differences, shortcomings of one or the other, distance due to military obligations, the family unit or marriage maintained its binds until "death do us part." Amazingly those firm believers of unity are slowly dying off. You rarely see a 75 plus year anniversary, nowadays your lucky to catch a 25. Divorce is just as quick and easy as going to Las Vegas and being married by Elvis, in some cases.

Both of my grandmothers were widows until the day they passed, at the same age of 83. My paternal grandmother was the typical apron-wearing, Sunday dinner, pastry baking, kind little old lady that most think of when they envision grandma. After marriage, having a child, the passing of her father, the sale of their family farm, then subsequently downsizing to a 4-bedroom home in suburbia, she went to work for the Thermos factory at an early age and retired from the same job at the age of 65. She married became a widow early on when my grandfather was tragically and critically burned as a spark ignited a fire while he was at the gas pump. The other tragic factor to this was that my father being nine years old at the time was a witness to this event. In 1947, the safety measures of today were not in place, and even now, a tragedy such as this one could still happen. From that day forward, my father, being the only child, began to receive preferential treatment, was enabled and catered to at every turn as he was looked at empathetically as the "poor child," which he learned to use to his advantage.

Baby boomers, on the other hand, pretty much cater to their children too much, further harming their ability to survive on their own. I have heard comments like, "I don't want my kids to have it as hard as I did," or "I want my kids to have a better life." How in the world is enabling, catering to, or Polly-coddling help your children succeed in life without you? I have yet to hear a logical response.

What I do know for a fact is that my primary influences came from the women in my life, as my mother did divorce my father, therefore being brought up in a single-parent household, I was stereotyped as being from a broken home and must have it hard. My mother worked, grandmothers both worked when I was young, and both were my babysitters as well.

In retrospect, I should be a full-bore liberal thinking woman with dominant female thoughts, which I am not, nor have I ever thought so. I looked at the world and those around me as the same. I don't care about what color you are, nationality, nor whether you are male or female. We all have strengths and weaknesses where our life experiences, religious, and educational backgrounds dictate our being. I have never been jealous of anyone because of what they have or what I wish I had instead. We all put our pants on the same way.

A fascinating aspect that I think of from time to time is the difference between my grandmother and her sister, my aunt, Thelma. My grandmother, who was widowed early, a single parent, worked, owned her house, had savings, was a go-to church every Sunday Lutheran woman. This woman didn't have a mean bone in her body that I had ever seen; she was kind to just about everyone she encountered. Although, there was a time or two, maybe more, when I got the back of my leg pinched and pretty darn hard at that, so that I would sit down and face forward in church. I liked to look to the back of the church to see who was coming in and wave to my friends, too much for my grandmothers wanting. I always wondered why we had to sit way up in the front. Those moments I guess you could say, I thought she was mean.

My aunt Thelma, on the other hand, was the, of the times, perceived typical, needed to be cared for subordinate female, rather high maintenance. Although she did get a job working at the factory alongside my grandmother, I learned later that it was basically to keep an eye on her and not leave her alone at home. My grandmother termed her as "high strung" or "sensitive." The story was told to me that she had married too young to a businessman who had a high paying job in New York, which required him to travel and stay there for days at a time. My aunt spent a great deal of time alone and never relocated to New York for fear of the city, which ultimately her husband began staying away for more extended periods, met another woman, and left her. This devastated her to the point that she began living in an altered reality. Not only was she left by the man of her dreams, but she was also now and dared it to be said back then, divorced, which my great-grandmother, her mother, was appalled by the very term.

As a young child, I remember the photo of my aunts, then ex-husband hanging on the wall in the living room. I will admit he was quite a looker. When I asked why this photo hung on the wall, my grandmother said it was to keep my aunt calm. My aunt never really spoke much to me or anyone else for that matter, barely to my grandmother. What I do remember is her daily routine of waking, having her breakfast prepared by my grandmother, she fixed her hair, dressed up as if going to church, only to sit on the 3-season porch every afternoon waiting for a man who never came. During the winter months, she would put on her heavy jacket and do the same, however, for less time as my grandmother would kindly go out and tell her some story to bring her back into the house. I was so young and curious. However, I knew not to ask questions when all was going well.

My maternal grandmother or memere was a bit different than my paternal grandmother. She was firm, outspoken, strong, and dominant in every aspect of her daily life. She was born in Caraquet, New Brunswick, Canada, in the middle of a cold January winter. The story was that she was destined to be a hellraiser by the way she survived. Born premature, she was placed in a shoebox, warmed in the oven until she was strong enough to move to the dresser drawer. With 13 children, I guess this was the best possible accommodations at the time. A determined baby to survive against the odds to a strong-willed child. Memere used to say it was the Mi'kmaq blood, not the Canadian that made her. When she was nine years old jobs became scarce, and the family realized it was time to venture out of Canada to the United States, settling first in Shirley, Massachussetts. With the sponsorship of family that had already come to the states for work on visas then becoming naturalized, opportunity was afforded easily to them to relocate.

Ultimately, my memere's relocation brought her to Norwich, Connecticut, under the sponsorship of my great uncle, she became naturalized and then met my grandfather, Pepe, married and had four children of her own.

Much like my paternal grandmother, memere too became widowed, however much later in her marriage than my grandmother. Her children already had children of their own; I was barely the age of 5 when my Pepe passed. I can still picture one of the last photos shown to me of my Pepe, where I stood on a chair next to him as he showed me how to baste the Thanksgiving turkey, that same turkey that would resemble the last Thanksgiving with him. He passed away unexpectedly in his sleep, next to my Memere. From that day forward sleeping in a bed was difficult for her, and she opted for her rest to be on the sofa.

As a child, I remember my Memere at every dance rehearsal, every town fair talent contest that I sang at, beach days, burgers at Kelly's or Lums, and the times she chased my cousin with the cat n' nine tails because he was sarcastic. She was barely 5' feet tall, far from mild. You knew when she was mad because half of what she said was in English the other half in French. Memere would tell a friend or stranger what she thought regardless, was active in the community, in the Catholic Church, and the lives of her children and especially her favorite grandchildren, luckily, I was one of them.

The strength and compassion I have today are by the learning and life experiences of others. The stories and actions of those dominant figures I viewed daily. Do I wish I had met my grandfathers? Absolutely. Do I feel that I have had something missing from my life? Not really, I have had so many opportunities and experiences; it doesn't feel that I am lacking. I am still learning and experiencing every day. I do wish to travel abroad more; however, with the unsettled times in the world, it doesn't seem probable yet.

The point to state is that my life experiences brought me to look at others the same, I did not need to feel a subordinate female to a man as my first figures were influential and sensitive without a male counterpart. Both owned their homes, worked their jobs, were community and church-oriented, raised their children, and thrived. Never did they nor I have an issue of suppression because we were women or subordinates. Perhaps it is or was a point of view never taught.

And from here, I must ask if we all could take a break in our lives and walk down memory lane, only briefly. Many of us can think back to our school age years and remember how exciting summer was and how agonizing to believe it was coming to an end. As kids, the last day of school meant, no more teachers, homework, and sleep in late, go to bed whenever was without rule. Some of us went to the shoreline with our families, stayed with our grandparents, or just hung out, without a care in the world.

Can you think of how seemingly simple life was? Remember the picnics, going to the beach and getting that awful first sunburn. Warm breezes, the faint sounds of summer with multiple radio stations playing, people laughing, swimming pool parties, or jumping off the dock at the pond for a cool off dunk in the water. I think back to the ease of making new summer friends at Misquamicut Beach in Rhode Island during the first couple weeks of summer vacation when our families would rent cottages and have such fun. Those strangers we met for the first time or saw only once a year when our families would be there at the same time were memories to last a lifetime. We cared less about where each other came from, how much money you had, did you believe in one thing or another, your parents were democrat or republican. No one cared, and neither did our parents or grandparents. We all had one common goal, have summer fun.

As I worked to finish this book another summer season had come and gone at the marina, I see it a bit differently than those days when I was a child playing on the beach in Rhode Island. However, being at the marina, you have a chance to meet and observe such a wide variety of people. Now that we are all adults, we have views, life experiences, and a wide range of opinions. The same still holds, all current event lunacy set aside, we all still want to have relaxation and summer fun.

The marina summer acquaintances mimic those of the past with each passing hello, we begin to enter into a new conversation of; fish tales, dive stories, and where the best places to dine are. Although marinas are technically the same, they all have boats attached to their docks or moorings. People stay on their boats overnight or go home. Some are seasonal, transients, or local boaters. They all have one thing in common, and what is most times are taken for granted, freedom, and something that happens each day with the rise and setting of the sun.

What I'm getting at here, is life sometimes needs to take a summer sabbatical. There are times when we all need to take a step back from our daily views, irritations, and criticisms. Breathe deeply, relax, and say to ourselves; we are all living the same life on this planet, no matter what our political viewpoint we need to work together even with our innate differences. Amazingly enough, whether we travel 1 mile or 100 miles to our floating getaway, or whatever getaway we have, we feel refreshed from our daily routine of irritation. Our aggression or frustrating political contradictions disappear. The everyday mundane boredom becomes boredom with a mind full of relaxation.

WHERE TO STOP

After all that has transpired during the election process, events, policy changes, obstructionist scenarios, hypocritical moments, positive turns, and negativities, I honestly could write every day about the seemingly never-ending Trump presidency saga. The sheer lunacy in our country has become, at times, a wonderment, whether the new ordinary reality is the idiocy or the wrong. In a country with such diversity, the ability for knowledge, advancement from poverty to wealth, it truly is astounding as to how we have become such a codependent nation rarely hearing the term "American dream." It used to be that the American dream was to finish school, go to college, get married, have a family, own a home, become financially successful. Now it appears the dream has taken on many new meanings straying away from the original thought process that most of us now middle-aged were brought up thinking.

We are in the age of titled millennials, 25 to 30 plus year-olds living at home with mom and dad, unable to find a suitable job to fund their desired way of life, or what mom and dad had made them accustomed to. Some feel that working a job in a fast-food restaurant is beneath them, they must get up too early if the requirement is before 10 am, or they must, dare I state it, do some form of physical labor. This paragraph falls into the same narrative as those that want to make their children's lives more comfortable than the viewed awful existence the parent had as a child. When does the time come when the baby bird is pushed from the nest to see it fly?

A 2018 court case came to light when 30 plus-year-old; Michael Rotondo, who was initially residing in his parent's house, on his parent's dime, not making the slightest effort to get a job, who needed to be evicted legally. As the media picked up the story and interviewed the newly removed freeloading child, he barely could fathom the reason why then commented in an interview that he guessed it was time to figure it out and get a job. Really? Growing up we were required to have a part-time job before we got our drivers license, you had a choice full-time job or college, some were lucky if their bags weren't packed waiting at the door for them to move out at 18. Generally, it was sink or swim by age 25.

Individuals that are known to us personally, both highly educated, good home, stable financially, active in the community, have children both of whom are college-educated. One still in college, the other a graduate who works the same introductory level job for the past 4 to 5 years with no apparent ambition to advance to management, step out into their college field of study, maintain the bare minimum. This young adult still lives at home and recently has refurbished the basement as a living space, subsequently moving in his new girlfriend of whom has little thought of advancement either. Yes, this is an example of what Hillary Clinton termed the Bernie Sanders supporters as basement dwellers. Ironically this family were supporters of Hillary Clinton during the 2016 election. How is this enablement going to teach survival without a never-ending full refrigerator of food, heat for warmth that magically happens without concern or lights that stay on without payment from mom or dad?

The sad part to the millennial umbilical cord cut-off is that they get angry with the parent, ultimately condemning them for their perceived hardships they have yet to incur, claiming abandonment. Some sadly never speaking to their parent or parents again and is an unfortunate event experienced by another close acquaintance as his children both did the very example I just set. Having been overly generous, wanting his children to have more than he, this man worked hard to provide a good home, cars, travel, monetary help, and educational advancements. Both yet to show any ability to maintain themselves independently, continued the parental enabled existence with the inevitable monetary plea for help that was consistently provided when asked for and rarely denied. He decided one day enough was enough and it was time. He stopped offering the free cars, paying for repairs, handing over cash for shortcomings, no more freebies. He had thought the years he had spent helping and providing for his children would be reciprocated with respect for all that he had done. Instead, he was met with hatred, contempt, and has not heard from either for years, even to the point that he has never met either of his grandchildren. Extreme? Yes. Pathetic? Absolutely. Although everyone has their reasoning, this example was surrounding a financial cut-off, the baby bird did not wish to fly. When does the support timeline end without inevitable recourse?

We are also in the age of DACA or the battle for the dreamers and not dreamers of our born or naturalized citizens but those of illegal aliens in our country who have taken political precedence over all others. Although many will state that my comments are heartless and uncaring at times, I and millions of others across the country firmly question this decision of the Obama administration. At what point did we turn a blind eye to the immigration laws of our country? As many of you already know, without my telling you, these "tagalongs" have more rights to dreams than natural-born or naturalized citizens.

Insight of the views of the lobbying Democrats, some Republicans and former President Obama, those born or naturalized citizen has plenty to spare. The battle continues, and the controversy still prevails. The Democrats in their obstruction resist movement opted to filibuster, halting the vote on spending because they wanted amnesty or citizenship for the DACA kids. Funding was held for CHIP or the Children's Health Insurance, Veterans, and government employees pay, all for the sake of illegals. Although the Trump administration offered a deal, it was turned down for political resistance sake and yet another compromise or pass the buck; the continuing resolution was reached that didn't include the illegals and America were released from being held hostage by our congressional lawmakers. Until next time, of course.

Amazingly enough, so many bloggers failed to understand that even though the Republicans technically held the majority of both the House and the Senate during this time, Democrat votes were still needed to meet the requirements to pass legislation and with this president, they will have no part of it, even if it helps the American people, as a whole.

Post 2018 mid-term elections, the #resist, obstructionist, new era Democrats managed to regain the House of Representatives the battle is far more an uphill climb. There shall be no give, no compromise, no matter the positive. Hypocrisy is the key to obstructionism when it comes to President Trump, his administration, and getting any commitment for the good of the American people from the Democrats.

I have always posed the questions to our lobbying senators and representatives, asking simply, why have these individuals not even attempted to become naturalized citizens of the country that has afforded them so much? Where are those individuals who allegedly brought these "tagalongs" across the border and have they become naturalized? Where are they? Many DACA individuals have not only prospered, are in college, considered minorities, therefore receiving grants and subsidies afforded by the US taxpayer. One would think that they would be gracious to become a proud naturalized citizen of the United States of America. Instead, they protest, burn our flag, call us racist, uncaring, and have the audacity to make demands. Quite ungrateful to say the least, wouldn't you say? Some Democrat leaders have termed these individuals as "America's children." What are legal children in America considered? As many protesting DACA act like spoiled brats, perhaps they need to lose privileges until they show some respect. Maybe in a perfect movie-like setting, but not in reality.

All this idiocy and unfair play, because millions of hardworking Americans want to fulfill their dreams first in the country that they were born to before others here illegally, now have become ungrateful and termed racial bigots. I have spoken to many naturalized immigrants of this country who are angered and disheartened just as much by the immigration failures or lack of enforcement. On Latino woman stated to us at the Trump rally, the primary reason she supported Trump was because of his views on illegal immigration. She went further to outline how "illegals" have ruined her life and made it harder for her. Another gentleman who emigrated from Greece, saved money for years just to come to America, was sponsored by his uncle, and became a naturalized citizen. He now drives other immigrants to New York periodically to accept their citizenship. Although it took this gentleman from Greece 17 years of his life to complete his goal, he was so proud to this day that he did, then, on the other hand, he is angered by the current immigration failures and status of illegals coming into the country.

Another hardworking woman from the Philippines, who I met in passing at a grocery store where she was the cashier, commented on my Trump 2020 hat that I was wearing, excitedly telling me that she had just renewed her green card. She went on to say how exhausting the immigration process was, from the application to the medical clearance. She went on to say how she really liked President Trump because he was for everyone and didn't like the people who come here illegally, it wasn't fair, and she worked only to have her taxes go to them. One would think if she thought I was a racist, she would not have been outwardly excited to speak to me that day.

Those few examples that I outlined previously in this chapter are the very examples of those who do not feel nor perceive Trump or his supporters as racists, bigots, or hate filled people. They were and are proud to have come to America, work hard and are unhappy with those illegal individuals in the country, polly-coddled by our governments bureaucratic politicians promoting the circumvention of laws and immigration processes.

Instead of obstruction, dragging of feet, circumvention, and alteration of meaning to our laws, the very lawmakers, placed in office, some for decades, should work together to close the migration and immigration loopholes. Many Democrats preach about rights and privileges of all citizens, they have lost track of their true constituency who are the very foundation that this country was built upon and themselves are fast becoming the tyrannical dictators attempting to control narratives or outcomes that we as a country escaped centuries ago.

Whether it be the ludicrous, immigration lottery program, temporary visa programs, DACA, chain migration, our immigration laws should be enforced. The days of the "warm and fuzzy" need to end. The Trump administration wants a substantial wall on the southern border or barrier that is not easily passable, stronger immigration enforcement of laws already in place and the closure of loopholes in the asylum, refugee, illegal alien visa expiration, and elimination of systemic failures.

Many Democrats hypocritically condemning illegal border entry in the past, today like or want open borders. Stated in an interview with The Arizona Republic, February 2018, then minority leader; Nancy Pelosi, "we need these people to mow the grass at the border" or "they do the jobs Americans won't do." Really? Many Democrats even lobby on illegals do the jobs that Americans won't do. Why is that?

New era Democrats appear to not want a part of any cure to our immigration problems, will obstruct, vote no, and vow resistance to anything the President or Republicans put forward.

Democrats have called for the abolishment of ICE agents, claiming them too brutal in their jobs. When is it enough for these obstructionist hypocrites who spoke out loudly in the past, lobbying for immigration enforcement, reform, and voting to approve border security funding including barrier walls and fences to enforce laws and end their hypocrisy? At what point will the resistance and obstructionism end just because it is President Trump who asks? How many more American Angel Families are needed to meet the quota for the supporters of the #resist movement, obstruct at all cost new era Democrats, to achieve the fictitious goal to work together and act on behalf of America first finally? When will it stop, when a Democrat like Beto O'Rourke is put in office who wants to tear down the current decades-old border or when a Socialism advocate like Bernie Sanders is seated at the checkbook writing bad blank checks that can't be funded?

Regardless, you don't have a country without laws and borders; even the Vatican in Rome has a wall, as well as Buckingham Palace which has a sturdy high fence with many guards. Need we forget about the Great Wall of China, now that's a wall. Why is it Democrats lobby for open borders, when we must be processed through customs when we return from vacation or go through security checkpoints, why are we subjected to this when illegals are not?

Now many will say that illegals do not vote; however, we all know they do and can accomplish this easily through the "motor voter" ID process. California instituted this process three days before the 2016 election, and surprisingly enough, California had the highest voter turnout for candidate Clinton. You will not see any absolute proof of citizenship for all those who voted, and California was the front runner to the citizenship question being removed from the governmental census questionnaire.

During the last presidential election, recounts were ordered in many states, finding altered ballots, walking dead voters, duplicate votes, multiple state votes for the same individual, and with these discrepancies, we as the American voter are not to believe there are not illegal citizens voting in our elections. I did find that amazing that so many dead people magically popped out of the ground across the nation to vote for Hillary Clinton, perhaps it was not the glass ceiling she was attempting to break but the confines of entombed. Well, I guess that would stand to reason as they probably had poor cable or satellite access underground and didn't get as lucky as so many other Americans who were influenced by Russia.

To date president-elect, Trump has completed so many tasks and pushed forward his campaign promises, even in the path of obstruction. He made promises to the American people of all political views that he has yet to receive credit for achieving many against political party obstruction and resistance. Even through adversity, criticism, ridicule, and condemnation, he trudges forward.

Another narrative in political propaganda play is his mental stability or lack thereof. Has anyone thoughtfully observed and listened to Nancy

Pelosi or Maxine Watters? Both of these women need to retire; however, the more they chatter, the more unhinged they sound further showing the American people where the Democrat party is headed. The same Democrat party that is more detached and far away from the American people, while contradictorily claiming to be #ForThePeople.

With the stock market doing well, typical ups and downs, job growth, more economic stability wavering more toward solvency versus bankruptcy, businesses are reinvesting into the country; you would expect to hear from the Democrats that we are all looking forward to working together with the President and Republicans to brighter days ahead. Not a chance, instead of from the mouth of the greatest obstructionists, Nancy Pelosi, states, "it is Armageddon," Democrat Maxine Watters chants the only words she seems to get excitement from, "impeachment" or "impeach 45". Well, at least Maxine Waters knows what president is in office and what number unlike her colleague Pelosi who has been heard more than once with the Freudian slip of; "President Bush." Nancy Pelosi herself or someone for her tweets regularly, and this is a common rebuttal tweet for me; "really Nancy"? As some of her comments and tweets are so disconnected and yes, lost in space somewhere.

The amount of rhetoric spewed consistently by so many in the media along with the fear promoting propaganda by disgruntled Democrats; I am amazed that we do not have more of a civil war between the left and right, as they are termed. The promotion of division is phenomenal. The worst division has been in race relations, as of late, which seriously we are peddling backward on. No matter the media outlet that you view, you will hear a consistent view of the racial divide. I found it ridiculous when this one guest for the conservative media outlets commented upon plowing in the fields. Now, this was an educated young black woman who I seriously doubt ever cultivated any fields; however, placed herself in a secondary level to white people. Sorry to inform her, having worked on a farm as a child, and now owning a farm, I, being a white, educated woman, have plowed the field and do not feel below anyone. Granted, with the help of modern technology and the 3-point attachment to the back of the tractor, it is much more comfortable. My point is that she nor I am any different other than by the pigmentation of our skin, or through the perception of our lives and family histories that may differ also. Unless I know this individual directly, have grown up with her, I can not specify one way or another, nor should she place herself in a stereotypical light of racism.

Much like the Douglas Democrats of the past that wanted segregation for the satisfaction of need based slavery, we as a fighting society are the Lincoln Republicans and Independents alike trying to maintain or regain decency, common ground, freedoms, and reel in a rogue government that we let slide for far too long.

Fact is, politicians have forgotten, look through us, refuse to hear anything other than the taxpayer funded jingle in their pockets. For us to unify as a nation, we need to step away from the D and R and concentrate on the I, Me, My, and We the people.

GUN CONTROL – A
STATE OF MIND

A day has yet to pass when we do not hear of another shooting death or be reminded of the mass shooting tragedies committed by an individual. The absent factors omitted from the narratives are always the same when put forward to the public or by those that lobby for gun control and suppression or removal of the rights under the second amendment. Rarely are facts presented that the individual who perpetrated the crime was known to have a history of mental illness, just over the legal age of being considered an adult or that there were failures on the side of law enforcement, database updates, and reporting by society or social media red flags.

With the progression in society and the blanket of the ACLU or privacy acts, an individual who should be followed, watched, or of concern is wrapped in a comfort blanket of red tape to surround them with rights of privacy. Every mass shooting in this country, with the exception to the Las Vegas massacre, were surrounded by this comfort blanket. Only a questioning security officer who viewed the numerous large bags being brought into the hotel by a short stay guest via the security footage, or inspections of every bag, every guest, every day by a security detail, may have hindered this event. Then again, a savvy guest or attorney would raise the offense that it was an invasion of a person and personal property. Only after an atrocity is committed can we see where the failures were, however, the failures and issues leading up to and surrounding the event must be acknowledged, not a single line item to push a political agenda.

In the case, Nikolas Cruz, a resident of Florida, of whom decided Wednesday, February 14th, 2018, was the day. He premeditated this event, prepared with an AR-15, pulled the fire alarm at the high school in Parkland, Florida, that he once attended and was expelled from prior. Knowing the dynamics, strengths, and weaknesses of his former high school, Nikolas Cruz began shooting as students exited the building, killing 17 and wounding many others both physically and emotionally.

As would be the case, the Senators, lobbyists and those opposed to guns were out in full force. One tweet came over the cyber highway of criticism, "Go, Gun Laws! Stupid conservatives!!!!!!!". Of course, feeling the need to respond to this illogical but opinion viewed comment my rebuttal was, "Laws are for law-abiding individuals, should the comment be stupid liberals for those guns used illegally?" Not to my surprise, there was no return comment.

Although the title "another bloody valentine" may seem a bit insensitive, creepy or sarcastic, the country has faced yet another Valentines' Day shooting. We can take ourselves back to the year 1929, where 7 persons, 5 of whom were known as the North Side Gang of Chicago, were gunned down, by the use, of the Thompson Submachine Gun or better known as the Tommy Gun, later changing gun laws, use, and ultimately no longer being produced. What was known to be the Valentines' Day Massacre which was committed by another rival gang over prohibition profits during an era of change.

Now we jump forward to Valentines' Day 2018 where 17 persons were killed, many more injured by a prior student who managed to purchase his firearm of choice a Colt manufactured semi-automatic AR-15, also known as an Armalite Rifle, not an assault rifle as many have been led to believe by the MSM and lobbying politicians. Firearms of both Valentines' Day atrocities have one similarity mass kill options, with great collateral damage but differed between hard to conceal versus easy to hide, heavy versus lightweight.

As with the Sandy Hook elementary school shooting in 2012 by Adam Lanza, of whom used a handgun with a high capacity magazine versus the AR-15, left in the trunk of the vehicle he drove to the school that day, he managed to inflict harm and death to many. Lanza started with his mother, shooting her multiple times, then on to defenseless children and adults, ultimately meeting his demise.

What is failed to be reported or acknowledged in the talking points of the MSM and legislators who lobby against the 2nd amendment are that in most cases, you had an individual who had been in the mental health system. Lanza was dropped by the system in oversight when he became 18 years of age, led a secluded life, and played violent shooting video battle games consistently. You hear little about this individuals' life, how he shot his mother numerous times, and in the face as being a psychological clue of overkill and anger, nor the probable cause and effect that may or may not have prevented this tragedy. Instead of looking at the root causes of a violent event, and inanimate object is made the blame.

The inanimate object rebuttal can be made with the Las Vegas shooter, Steven Paddock, who utilized a modification unit called a bump stock, which enabled rapid repetitive firing without the need for human action to cause the firearm to fire. In this case, it was the inanimate object that caused multiple acts of harm; however, without the human intervention that inanimate object would not have been made, nor attached by the perpetrator. We may never know why Steven Paddock chose that day, time, hotel, or location. He showed no reported signed of activism, retaliation, social media outcries, or was in the mental health system at one point. He passed his background checks, made his purchases without issue, and appeared average and typical.

Las Vegas, in addition to multiple shooting deaths over the decades with Columbine, San Bernardino, Pulse Nightclub, Sandy Hook, Parkland, all have one thing in common, the shooter, the enabler. Legislators like Chris Murphy (D) of Connecticut, called for gun-free zones, which the term itself welcomes a shooter who wishes to cause as much destruction without the fear of immediate retaliation. As with all mass death or destruction scenarios, the perpetrator knows the area, makeup, security aspects, and systematic responses as proven examples are seen in each event. The premeditation may take days, hours, or years to formulate, and only the psyche of the individual knows how, why, and when.

After every unfortunate shooting anti-gun groups and campaigning politicians try to advocate to remove the rights of all American citizens to protect themselves by bearing arms, further places them at risk to potentially be harmed at some point in time when that one psyche decides it is now, it's a poor choice by those who lobby for the constitutional change.

The NRA, political scene, lobby groups, and advocates are always on the rampage. Legal gun owners are fearful of their constitutional, right to bear arms, and the probability of losing that right, if the legislation passes. One of the platforms that then-candidate Trump ran on was the belief in the Constitution and the 2nd amendment rights of all legal U.S. citizens.

Which believably was one of the reasons he had such a great deal of support from many conservatives and those in the midline of political views.

For every neglected detail left out by propagandist politicians seeking to suppress the 2nd amendment rights, there are multiple reasons and factual data to support leaving it alone and find a solution to the human root problem. Although not one of us will know the actual reasoning behind every mass casualty, we all know one thing, if a firearm is involved, the 2nd amendment will be on the table. In an effort to see both sides of the aisle or point of view, I find myself asking the question why is such a firearm like the AR-15 necessary to the gun owner? Is it vital to possess any large capacity or firearm capable of causing mass casualties like those by the action of the AR-15 or the "Tommy Guns" of the past? Unless we must foresee the need to kill off zombies in large numbers, this should be something we all should know or be made aware of perhaps.

Our founding fathers had the forethought and belief that the people of the United States should have the same abilities as the government in the event of a necessary overthrow, or when the government ceased to work for the people. The right to bear arms of the day was written when all were on a level playing field as it could be when it came to firearms. With modern-day advancements and alterations throughout the years, it still holds true, except for nuclear bombs, where the average citizen does not necessarily have. Military-grade firearms are not only in the hands of the government but in the hands of the citizens as well. Unfortunately, not all are level minded, law-abiding individuals.

With the volatile social atmosphere that we have had bubbling for some time over the past decade or so, the volcano finally erupted with another shooting by an anti-Semitic individual who killed 11 and injured many others in a Pittsburgh, PA synagogue during the Shabbat morning service. Without warning, the alleged gunman at the time of this writing was Robert Gregory Bowers, who admitted guilt and stated he intended to "kill these people" in his anti-Jewish, anti-Semitic rants. Of course, the blame was placed on President Trump because he has been depicted as anti-Semitic, even though he was the president who finalized the move of the American Embassy to Israel acknowledging Jerusalem when his predecessors failed to do so. His daughter Ivanka and son-in-law, Jared, were practicing Jews, with Jared being a descendant of Holocaust survivor grandparents.

The MSM, political talking heads, and social media were ablaze with accusations and the casting of blame. The hypocrisy of many was the acquaintance to the decades-old outspoken anti-Semite Louis Farrakhan who has many a time referred to Jews as evil. Farrakhan lavished in the thought of being referenced to Adolf Hitler and had even preached he took joy in being called anti-Semitic making a mockery by twisting the term to state, "I have been told I am an anti-Semite, no I am anti-termite."

Not one that I interacted with, nor was there any media call out, leftist or democrat politicians' condemnation, even in the wake of this tragedy. As with all tragedies, the root problem was not the individual themselves. More emphasis was placed on the president and his family showing their respects, viewed by the MSM and propagandist politicians as hypocritical because the narrative needed to be upheld that Trump was anti-Semitic.

So then, as the number of mass shootings has been increasing, is it the firearm or the shooter? As a firearm cannot think for itself, act on its own, nor operate without human interaction on some level, a logical person would say the problem is the shooter. Another, less rational-minded, or politically motivated individual will argue, the fault of the gun.

A question to ask when the debate arises would be that of planes. As 9/11 was caused by planes crashing into buildings, flown by terrorists to cause harm to our country, were the deaths of those 2,996 and more than 6,000 injured the fault of the plane or the pilot? Should we lobby for the ban on aircraft?

Hours, days, months, years, we are all still in the debate, ban guns, gun control, more regulations. However the fact remains, in the cases of; Sandy Hook, Connecticut, Adam Lanza and the case of Nikolas Cruz, what we do know is that each previously mentioned reached the legal age of an adult, had a history of mental illness or outbreak and had fallen through the cracks in the mental health continuing care system.

Years ago, as an EMT, one of our primary functions was to transport back and forth to the Norwich State Hospital. I am curiously wondering, each time I pass this now vacant location, with its broken windows, buildings being torn down to build another casino owned property, I cannot help but ask, "Where did they all go?". Has our progression in civil liberties and acts of privacy caused the demise of many other lives because we have failed to monitor or maintain connections to those with proven, documented, and observed mental improprieties or instabilities? Have we become a society that looks through rose-colored glasses, or with tunnel vision, failing to see what is truly before us? All questions quickly answered and applied differently to every probable scenario.

Granted, we cannot allow ourselves to get into the stereotype views of someone who acts oddly in our opinion; however, in the cases of Lanza and Cruz, evidence was documented and not maintained as concerning or flagged. In the cases of; San Bernardino, the Pulse Night Club, and Sutherland Springs, all were flagged, forgotten, or overlooked by a broken reporting system. Perhaps Las Vegas could be seen as boredom or lack of necessity to be critical.

Regardless, the battle for the rights of individuals to bear arms shall be a political battle for decades to come until one political party or the other concedes the battle on behalf of the people.

Recently, a National Emergency was instituted by President Trump to enable funding for the southern border wall completion project. Not only has this border security issue been a part of each administration for the past few decades, but it was also another battle of obstruction and resistance by the new era democrat party. Moments after the announcement of the National Emergency, the social media tweets, and political podium threats began to set the stage for the time when a Democrat president would be dually elected to office, and the 2nd amendment or gun control would be called out as a National Emergency. More of a tit-for-tat moment.

Gun laws can be enhanced; background checks can be made more difficult, more fees, fines, or conditions can be placed upon law-abiding gun owners or those that wish to become gun owners. Not one more law shall prevent the illegal purchase, use, or modification by an individual who wants to harm themselves or others. The maintenance of the right to bear arms as set forth by the 2nd amendment is the duty of the voter. Therefore, if we as voters wish to keep or change anything, it is up to us to make sure the politician that lobbies to constrict our constitutional rights is removed from office or never swears an oath to "allegedly" uphold that office. It is our right as citizens to protect ourselves and others when another seeks to harm, if the person wishing to harm is armed, we should be able to defend ourselves on the same plane. Common sense would tell you if one has a loaded gun aimed at you, the likelihood you will win the battle with a newspaper ready to swat at them like a fly will be moot.

The classic example, if the legal gun owner had not fired upon Devin Patrick Kelley, the shooter in Sutherland Springs on November 5, 2017, the massacre would have been much more significant. This brave Samaritan took his firearm, shot, hitting Kelley twice, causing him to flee the scene instead of reloading and returning inside the First Baptist Church to kill more than the 26 people already dead and injuring more than the 20 he already had, the numbers would be quite different. Not only was Kelley an individual not adequately recorded in a failed database which is supposed to contain the pertinent information to deny the purchase of a firearm during a background check, he suffered documented mental break issues that were not being followed up on by another broken system.

Lobbying politicians or the MSM do not calculate all system failures, societal issues, privacy concerns, and legal versus illegal values, are only an effort to mislead by way of emotion to change, eliminate, or suppress the constitutional rights of a nation. This very act is unconstitutional intent by those politicians and MSM, only by the diligence of the people will their efforts be thwarted. This battle will never be over and can never be taken lightly or for granted.

CONCLUSION

Once thankful that Tuesday, November 6th, 2018, finally arrived. No more media propaganda in the mailbox, no more campaign signs blown over, strewn along the roadside, the voting day had finally arrived, only to be inundated once again by the next round of tree-killing propaganda.

We heard of the blue wave, red tide, blue tsunami, red wave, it all depended upon the voter response to the political rhetoric. Would the pollsters be correct this time, and the Democrats would take over the house and senate? Would Nancy Pelosi become or remain a speaker of the House of Representatives? Would the Trump effect retake control, with all those named racist, homophobic, misogynistic, deplorable smelly Walmart people come out and vote?

In 2018 as the votes came in and the final counts certified, it was apparent that the Democrats would again gain the House; however, the Republicans would increase in the Senate. What would be realized a short time into the new elections that the incoming freshman politicians would include more radical left thinking that the country could not afford and what would fast be seen to be potentially dangerous to our societal safety, unity, and progression.

Although these pages could continue filled with paragraphs of opinion, one must ask themselves, have we progressed, or have we been made to believe that we have? Are we all that different, you and I? We are biologically made up of living cells, deemed by chromosomes male or female in gender, with or without a womb to bear children or the sperm to impregnate. We all bleed red if injured, cry in pain when hurt. Only is it the location of our birth, pigmentation changed over the centuries to accommodate our surroundings, does this make us seem different on the outside. Throughout history, we as a people have battled each other relentlessly, whether it be by religious beliefs, retaliation for misconceptions, misinterpretations of words said or written, or mostly the lack of respect for and understanding of one another.

One factor that appears to hold is those who take advantage of others for personal gain or control. There have always been the supreme and the subordinates. Generally, those subordinates were less educated purposely so as not to allow an equal plane of thought, therefore loosening the reigns of control. Those reigns grasped tightly by those who felt they were above all, enslaving others to do their bidding, allowing them to remain seated above or looked upon as supreme.

When someone is asked to define slavery, the immediate reference answer for many in this country are always black slaves captured and brought here to be sold; meaningless individuals looked upon as inhuman. The reality is that slavery or enslavement is no longer specific to one ethnicity, race, or country of origin. Fact is, means of enslavement show examples to us from which we must awaken ourselves to the reality while we pay our taxes, feed our families, work our jobs not because we find pleasure in doing so, but we must survive in this monetary society that we have created for ourselves.

There is an element of social acceptance that enslaves many in their desire to be accepted by others or appear more than they are. We are allowed some pleasures to keep us happy such as owning a home, driving our cars, traveling where we wish within our country. However, these and all simple pleasures come at a price as we must pay a mortgage or tax on our land and homes. We are taxed on what we buy, we pay tax to own our cars, we pay tolls and fines when in our cars for travel, and we have boundaries we must not cross as we do not belong or have the privilege to do so.

We may speak when allowed, and if our speech is in opposition to those who listen or if it holds any truth in contradiction, we are suppressed and silenced. We must demand that all who live in this country play an active part in keeping our politicians, talk show commentators, educational facilities, and media outlets accountable. These figureheads must be held to a high standard for all they do and say as they are considered the supreme in many easily influenced eyes of admiration, causing us as a nation not to progress as a people but stalemate as a human body. Those not held accountable are causing our society to implode upon itself, lady justice is no longer blind but now sees through a transparent blindfold casting favor upon those placed on a higher threshold causing the scales to tip unfairly.

Another societal longstanding negative to Hillary Clinton's campaign or her presidential campaign of 2016, became the creation of a stereotyped people no longer the people in unity, "one nation under God," it became "the people" or "those people." Anyone who dares to speak out against the Democrat party agenda for the first woman in the office to follow the first black man in the office was forever scorned and shunned from the "it takes a village," village.

Even after years past young adults and families who dare to speak out with what is considered conservative values and thoughts are publicly castrated, humiliated, are a party to divisive propaganda with threats and violence. We have fast become not a country of laws, but a dictatorship with a poisoned army conditioned in thought by a generation of indoctrination.

With all the fear-mongering and claims the end is near, one would think that there would be a high number of suicide attempts. With the polarization of our country, the division began to widen even more with the candidates' political propaganda, blame game, and hypocrisies at an all-time high. We are inundated with Hollywood and musicians dictating or presenting us with suggestive reasoning why we should or should not vote for a candidate based upon their messaging against the Trump administration. It is apparent that it was not only Hillary Clinton who had not come to the reality of losing the 2016 election but millions of others who could not accept that they were not all-knowing and essential enough to persuade millions to accommodate their political beliefs or desires.

Granted, this saga shall continue and "We the People," deplorable as we all may be, we will need to maintain to stand for our freedoms. We need not stand for freedoms to condemn others because they are different, but the freedoms to coexist indifference. The desperate need for the people to take the time, be diligent, pay close attention to the political rhetoric is more crucial now than ever before in our lifetime.

We have a New Era Democrat driving force that is tearing away at the very core of our freedoms. The proposed changes and propagated divisions are unalike those seen during the 2016 presidential race. We have a political campaign reproducing racism when none exists, thwarted outward perceptions of hate when there is none. And most of all, control hungry propagandists dangerously seeking to divide the country through the "race card" dealing it at every hand when one is questioned.

Even the staunch Democrats, Union workers, minorities, should ask themselves, "why do they keep asking for change on the same subjects

187

that the Democrats promised to correct?" Why is the Democrat party continuously calling for unity when their rhetoric is divisive and why do they lobby for equality when their actions and words speak racism against all others? Another curiosity could be, whereas the Democrat party that once promoted for immigration enforcement of laws and border control now protects illegal aliens or undocumented persons in the country while ignoring the safety and needs of their constituency?

The 2020 stage has been set, and the actors are in play. It is up to the people of the USA, whether they vote for their freedoms, livelihoods, constitutional rights, and American patriotism or if they choose the New Era Democrat form of America. The extreme left-wing politician's platform is the right of the world and not a separate country for its legal citizens; politicians held unaccountable for their double standards of justice, higher taxation for the liberty to survive and pay for the rest of the worlds needs before your own and government control over every aspect of your lives.

Your vote matters people, and it is a right you should not take for granted. Keep in mind, if the Democrats are pandering to illegal immigrants, undocumented citizens, and illegal aliens, they are finding a way to get them into the voting box. Although this comment may seem a conspiracy theory, you must ask why the rights and needs of legal Americans are second to the world?

Hence, to be continued.

Printed in the United States
By Bookmasters